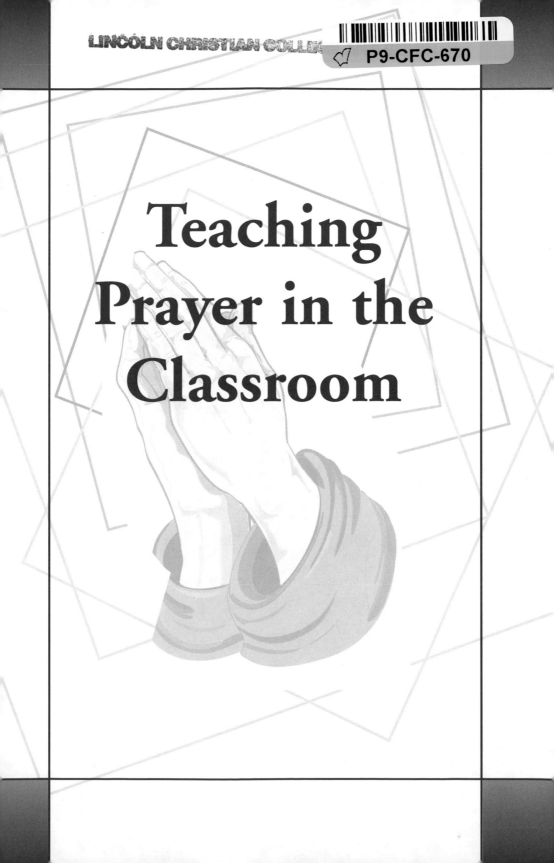

Teaching Prayer in the Classroom

Teaching Prayer in the Classroom

Experiences for Children and Youth

Revised and Expanded

Delia Halverson

Abingdon Press
Nashville

TEACHING PRAYER IN THE CLASSROOM
EXPERIENCES FOR CHILDREN AND YOUTH

Copyright © 1989 by Abingdon Press
Revised and expanded edition—Copyright © 2003 by Abingdon Press

This book is printed on acid-free paper.

Library of Congress Cataloging-in-Publication Data

Halverson, Delia Touchton.
Teaching prayer in the classroom : experiences for children and youth
/ Delia Halverson—Rev. and expanded.
   p. cm.
Includes bibliographical references.
   ISBN 0-687-06425-2
   1. Prayer—Christianity—Study and teaching. 2. Christian education of children. 3. Christian education of young people. I. Title.

BV214.H26 2003
268'.432—dc21

2003004481

Unless otherwise noted, all scripture quotations are taken from the Good News Translation in Today's English Version—Second Edition Copyright © 1992 by American Bible Society. Used by permission..

Scripture quotations marked (CEV) are from the Contemporary English Version, © 1991, 1992, 1995 by American Bible Society. Used by permission.

Scripture quotations marked (RSV) are taken from the Revised Standard Version of the Bible, copyright 1946, 1952, 1971 by the Division of Christian Education of the National Council of the Churches of Christ in the United States of America. Used by permission. All rights reserved.

Those marked (KJV) are from the King James Version of the Bible.

03 04 05 06 07 08 09 10 11 12—10 9 8 7 6 5 4 3 2 1

MANUFACTURED IN THE UNITED STATES OF AMERICA

Contents

108330

Introduction

"Now I lay me down to sleep; I pray the Lord my soul to keep."

For many of us this was the first prayer we learned. I recall as a child not liking the words I was taught for the second sentence to this prayer: "If I should die before I wake, I pray the Lord my soul to take." It held mysteries I didn't care to explore. Thankfully, new words have been coined for this prayer that refer to sleeping through the night and waking with morning light instead of dying.

Teaching children and youth to pray can be challenging. Or perhaps I should say it can be intimidating. Consequently we often ignore it. As parents, we may say, "That's the church's job." As classroom teachers, we may simply ignore the opportunities, hoping that another teacher will feel more comfortable with prayer.

In teaching children and youth, you will have to deal with every student's past experiences with prayer. Some will come from homes where prayer is a natural part of family life. Some will have learned classroom prayers. Others will bring no prayer experiences into the classroom at all. It is even likely that you will have a student who has never heard the word *prayer*.

Parents can sometimes get so caught up in the rush and struggle to fit everything into a schedule that they ignore opportunities to experience prayer personally, let alone with their children. This is the challenge of developing spirituality in the home in today's world. However, as teachers, we can be deliberate in helping parents recognize opportunities to experience prayer with their children. At the end of each of the first four chapters I have included information titled "Prayer at Home" that may be reproduced for parents' use. Please read each sheet before reproducing it since most refer to several chapter activities, charts, and so forth, that will also need to be reproduced and attached.

Whether in the classroom or in the home, as teachers of the faith, we have the responsibility of creating an atmosphere that enables children and youth to grow in their relationship with God. Faith is a response to our relationship with God. Our beliefs may change and vary as we grow through life experiences. The relationship with God can begin at an early age and mature in a very personal way.

Often we feel that our main objective is to teach the Bible and information about the Bible or beliefs that are compatible with our denomination. But unless children and youth learn to apply what they learn to their daily lives and develop a relationship with God that is the heart of their faith, what they learn remains impersonal. All of the "knowledge" becomes, as Paul's statement to the Corinthians says, as only "a noisy gong or a clanging cymbal" (1 Corinthians 13:1 RSV). The personal relationship between a person and God becomes the artery for that love to develop, and prayer is the muscle of that artery.

Often, as I lead workshops and seminars for parents and teachers across the country, I am asked, "How can I help my children pray?" Many people feel that their own prayer lives are inadequate, and are afraid to pray with children and youth. Prayer is simply talking to God. Just as our conversations with a new friend become more comfortable as our friendship matures, our prayers (or conversations) with God will become more comfortable as we seek out those opportunities to speak to God and develop that friendship.

Children and youth learn more frequently by our modeling than by our instructions. This book is designed to help you find ways to model prayer and to guide children and youth in developing their own conversations with God.

Chapter 1

What Is Prayer and How Do We Begin?

How do we begin? We begin at the beginning. The simpler we make prayer, the better. In years past, the primary prayers of the church were formal expressions, using eloquent words. Many people assume that praying is something they cannot do because they often only hear polished prayers from the pulpit, and because our hymnals and books of prayer contain such formal prayers. Prayers with eloquent words began as prayers from the heart. However, when we take someone else's words and repeat them often or if the words are not natural to us, we sometimes close our minds to the meanings of such prayers. Simple prayers from the heart are just as effective as, or may be more effective than, a written prayer that has been passed down to us from our church heritage. Every one of us has inwardly prayed a simple prayer at some time when we had a great need to communicate with God. It may have been something as simple as "God, give me strength!" These prayers are heard by God just as personally as those from the pulpits of churches.

It has been suggested that memorized or traditional prayers are like practicing swim strokes on the edge of a pool. The practice is important, but until we let ourselves get into the water and feel it uphold and support us, we cannot experience true swimming. Until we begin to wade out into the person/God relationship that we call prayer, we cannot experience true praying.

Praying is a conversation with God. A friend of mine who is now a mature Christian young lady began having simple conversations with God when she was two years old. I recall a time when she and her mother had lunch with me on our back deck. In her simple conversational tone, Jana told God the different things that we had before us to eat. Then she told God about her plans for the afternoon. As she closed, she simply said, "That's all. Amen." Even at such a young age, she ministered to me, an adult. Her prayer contributed to my own growth in faith.

We grow as we know and interact with children. Our growth, in turn, models our faith to the children. We are in this faith journey together—children, youth, and adults—sharing our God-relationship with one another. If we want to help children and youth grow in prayer, we must first be in prayer ourselves. We need to pray in order to grow in our personal relationship with God, and we need to pray for our children and youth daily while working with them. Adapt the following prayer calendar to your own situation. As a teacher, you can pray for your class by dividing your students among the five weekdays. Parents can place the names of their children and other family members on the days of the week. Use the calendar each day during prayer time.

God, Our Personal Friend

Prayer develops a friendship with God. When you meet a new person that you would like to have as your friend, how do you go about developing that friendship? You do not pull out some sort of prewritten words that talk about friendship and relationships and stand before the person reciting the words. You try to find out all that you can about that person, and you reveal yourself to that person so that you can appreciate the opinions and experiences you have in common.

If God is to be our personal friend, then we must approach God as we would approach a new friendship. We must express our appreciation, we must share our everyday experiences, and we must be open in all that we do and all that we think.

There is a story of a young boy who stood at the study door, looking at his father. When the father finally real-

PRAYER CALENDAR

Thank God for all your students and allow your love for them to EXPLODE!	Praise God!	Sunday
	Pray For:	Monday
	Pray For:	Tuesday
	Pray For:	Wednesday
	Pray For:	Thursday
	Pray For:	Friday
Your Church and your work with children and youth, and allow God to work through you. Share God's grace	Pray For:	Saturday

Type	Definition	Points
Adoration	Prayer whereby we are in awe of God.	• More than awe over such things as an atom, it is a worshipful awe whereby look to God for strength and help. • It involves a personal relationship with God. • It looks for thanksgiving opportunities throughout the day. • Like "lookin' and lovin' God." • In response to the personal love that we feel from God, we offer a personal love back to God and toward others.
Confession	Prayer whereby we meet God and accept the whole truth about ourselves.	• Confession is difficult without having experienced adoration. • Sin is our separation from God. (See the question about sin on page 25.)
Thanksgiving	Prayer whereby we recall things for which we are thankful.	• These are beginning prayers for young children. • They may be spontaneous or planned. • Consider *all* we have for which to be thankful, including disappointments and failures that help us grow. • The joy of thanksgiving helps us enter into a creative partnership with God.
Supplication	Prayer whereby we give our wants and desires over to God.	• Petition without pressure, but surrender. • It is sort of a junior/senior partnership with God, in which the junior partner recognizes needs, and the senior partner is aware of the needs and helps the junior partner grow in achieving those needs.

ized that he was there, he asked the boy, "Can I do something for you?" The boy answered simply, "Nope. I'm just lookin' and lovin'." Times of simply looking and loving are also important as children develop their prayer relationship with God.

Sometimes we can better understand prayer if we look at the different types or elements in our prayers. The remainder of this chapter will discuss prayers of *adoration, confession, thanksgiving, supplication*, and *intercession*.

The ACTS of Prayer

By using the word *ACTS*, we can remember four important elements in our prayer life. At the end of this chapter you will find suggestions for ways to help students learn these words and definitions.

Adoration
Confession
Thanksgiving
Supplication

From early biblical times there is reference to the "fear of God." For biblical people this phrase did not hold the same meaning that we connect with the word *fear* today. The biblical writer used this word when speaking of the "awe" of God.

Supplication is a word seldom used now. *Petition* is another word for this act of prayer; however, because the current use of the word *petition* usually involves applying pressure for change, we often get the wrong idea about the meaning of petitions in a prayer. Pounding away at God does not make for a creative partnership. In the following story, two people come to God in prayer in two different ways.

> Bob was a . . . member of our church some years ago when he discovered he had cancer. His wife attended and participated in programs, but she did not have Bob's spiritual

depth. Their teenage daughters were in the youth group. As Bob's fight against cancer progressed, his wife sought spiritual help elsewhere. She found a church that gave her a special formula for prayer and told her with that formula and deep faith, Bob would be healed.

When healing did not take place, Bob's wife blamed it on his lack of faith and divorced him. Her church encouraged her to "rid herself of the stumbling block in her own faith." The teen daughters were forced to decide between their mother, who believed that she had found new spiritual understanding, and their father, who was dying of cancer but could petition God for the help he needed to deal with his stressful situation, still holding onto the love that he knew God gives.

The teenage girls had two types of petition prayers, or prayers of supplication, modeled for them. The mother petitioned God to be on her side, healing so that she might have a physically whole husband. The father's petition gave him the ability to be in tune with God as a partner in his life. Even though the father was not healed physically, his petition released his body and mind so that he could be on God's side, establishing a partnership with God. He received the inner healing that helped him through the final months of his life.[1]

The youth in this story experienced two different models and were forced to make choices and judgments that were difficult. We model Christian lifestyles in our prayers as well as in our living. What messages are we sending to others? There are times when it is important to help children and youth recognize that we are all working through our own faith journey, and that what is important in that journey for one person may be different for another.

When we recognize our needs and petition God, we realize that God is in control of the world and of our lives. We give our wants and desires over to God instead of pleading with God to "come over to our side." Prayer is not a matter of playing sides and persuasion, but a matter of creative partnership. When we realize that God is in charge, our prayers of supplication will reflect this.

Jesus modeled supplication for us when he prayed, "not my will, but thine, be done" (Luke 22:42 KJV). God will give us strength and insight to live our lives as effectively as possible.

Prayers of Intercession

God created us to be in relationship with others. We express that relationship through intercessory prayer. First John 4:20 tells us that the acts of loving God and loving others are natural partners. This God-created relationship with others makes intercessory prayer natural.

Lance Webb, in his book *The Art of Personal Prayer,* described intercessory prayer as loving another person in God. It is a loving surrender of the other person to God—just "showing" God the person and your love for that person. It is not a magical force to get the person to "change," but a loving relinquishment of the other person, whether that person changes or not, and acknowledging to God that we relinquish the person with no strings attached. It's hard because we do this for a while, then we quite naturally pull the person back again.

True intercessory prayer lifts the burden off our shoulders and puts it in God's hands. If we try to "persuade" God by praying properly and for the correct amount of time, then we keep the burden on our shoulders. Intercessory prayer is like lending our minds and hearts out to God, but this requires a surrender of our will. When we pray in an act of giving-over rather than of asking, we find release.

Praying for others seems to be universal and a part of the depth of our nature. Just as the forces of electricity were in the world from the beginning of our world, and it took discovery of its source and channels in order for us to use it, God created and set up channels or paths for us to love and care for one another. Discover intercessory prayer and you will discover channels that connect you with other people. Without intercessory prayer our world is simply wound up to run. Prayer completes the circuit.

Webb suggests three steps in praying for others:
(1) Wait in the presence.
(2) Be willing to give yourself.
(3) Give the one for whom you pray to God.[2]

In praying even for those who persecute us (as Jesus taught in Matthew 5:44), we are also changed. We see the person for whom we are praying as God sees that person. The situation and relationship changes so that God can act. Prayer sets the stage and opens us to God's guidance.

When we live our prayers, then our prayers and life are one. Sometimes we never know what effect our prayers have on the other person. In intercessory prayer, spiritual victory happens whether the physical and immediate outcome is what we expected or not. Physical healing without spiritual healing is useless in our ministry for God.

Helping Children and Youth Identify Prayers

Younger children will take part in some of the elements of prayer, particularly in adoration and thanksgiving. Older preschool and younger elementary children can begin to deal with confession because it is personal. Most older elementary children and youth can grasp some understanding of prayers of supplication or petition. Simple prayers of intercession may be used at a variety of ages, such as asking God to be with the doctors who are helping a sick friend.

Although you may not want to introduce all of the "ACTS" elements of prayer or the term "intercessory prayer" until children are of middle to late elementary age, you can find many times to point out specific types of prayer as you use them.

Help younger children recognize prayers of adoration or thanksgiving by using the terms before or after you pray. This can be done by saying, "Let's pray a thanksgiving prayer for our food (friends, parents, flowers, and so forth)." Or you might say, "When I see the tiny ants that God created, I know we have a great God. Let's say a prayer that tells how we adore God."

Children who can understand telling someone "I'm sorry" can realize that confessing is telling God that we are sorry, and we can begin to name such prayers.

In the chapter on creating personal prayer, I suggest that students learn to bring people who are special into their hearts in prayer. As you talk about such prayers with older children and youth, explain that sometimes we call these types of prayers intercessory prayers.

There are many possible methods to help older students learn the types of prayers. The best way is to mention the type as you use the prayer. If we begin teaching prayer by simply talking about the "types" of prayers, we can create confusion. Students need plenty of experience with first being submersed in prayer. Teaching types of prayer without praying would be like learning the alphabet before learning to speak. After working with prayer in your classroom, and when the students feel comfortable in many prayer situations, use some of the methods below to help them learn to identify prayers.

Activities for Learning Different Types of Prayers

1. Using some of the prayers of our heritage found in chapter 5, help students identify the prayers or parts of prayers that are of adoration, confession, thanksgiving, supplication, or intercession.

2. Create matching games by putting sentence prayers and types of prayers on individual cards. These either can be paired up or can be used for a concentration game. Here is an example:

God, the power of a waterfall amazes me.	Prayer of Adoration
I'm sorry that I hit Joe.	Prayer of Confession
Thank you, God, for the rain.	Prayer of Thanksgiving
God, I've studied, but help me with the test.	Prayer of Supplication
I want to help Jane, God. She's unhappy.	Prayer of Intercession

3. Place on a bulletin board the letters **A, C, T, S,** and **I.** Assign groups or individuals to write appropriate prayers for each letter—prayers of adoration for the letter "*A*," prayers of confession for "*C*," and so forth. Post the finished prayers. Use them at appropriate times during the class, such as to open or close the session or as a litany during a worship time.

4. Initiate a prayer chain. When there is someone who needs prayer, begin the chain by calling one of the students and mention the type of prayer that is appropriate. That student calls another to pass on the message, and so on, through the class.   Whatever methods you use with your class, it is important to help the students feel at ease with prayer and not apply pressure. Prayer is personal, and although we want our children to grow in their ability to share their prayers with others, we also want to keep it at a personal level.

PRAYER AT HOME

What Is Prayer and How Do We Begin?

In today's world, we find less and less time to involve our children in organized religious training, and so it is important that we grasp every opportunity possible to live out the faith for our children. Faith is not a particular set of beliefs. Faith is our relationship with God. As we grow and mature, our beliefs may change, but our relationship with God can deepen. To do this, prayer must become an ongoing experience wherever we are and no matter what we are doing.

Establishing prayer in the home is fundamental to sharing our faith with children and youth. Every parent and caregiver yearns to give their children the best possible foundation for their understanding of God. But we are often baffled as to how to begin. Many of us grew up with very formal prayers, and we feel inadequate about praying. Prayer need not be a complicated procedure. *In simple words, prayer is conversation with God.* Just as you cannot have a firm relationship with another person without conversation, prayer builds our relationship with God. The attached chart on ACTS may help you with your own prayer life.

Children and adults are in this faith journey together, and you will grow in your own relationship with God as you share in conversations about prayer and as you pray together. This can all begin with your own personal prayers. Place the names of your children and other relatives on the prayer calendar attached to this sheet and use it regularly in your own prayer time.

God created us and seeks a personal relationship. If God is to be our personal friend, then we must approach God as we would approach a new friendship. We must express our appreciation, we must share our everyday experiences, and we must be open in all that we do and all that we think.

Attachments:
Prayer Calendar
A.C.T.S.

Chapter 2

Questions About Prayer Most Often Asked

Everyone who has worked with children and youth knows that they are filled with questions. Indeed, we too have questions from time to time. Even Jesus, in his final prayer on the cross, asked, "My God, my God, why have you forsaken me?"

There is no way that we can know all of the answers, and there is no reason to be embarrassed when we cannot answer a question. The best answer is sometimes to ask "And what do you think?" This allows an opportunity to inquire into the questioner's beliefs. It is also appropriate to say "Let's do some research and find out what others think about that."

Here are some common questions asked about prayer, and my personal answers. Reflect on these and then decide on your own responses.

Why Do We Bow Our Heads and Close Our Eyes When We Pray?

We need not have specific body positions for prayer. When you are driving down a busy highway and feel a need to ask God for guidance, do you pull over to the side of the road and get down on your knees to pray? Praying is a living communication with God, and the sooner children and youth realize that, the more at home they will feel in prayer.

There are two reasons for us to bow our heads and close our eyes in prayer: (1) *to block out the distractions around us,* and (2) *to humble ourselves.* Young children cannot understand the abstract concept of being humble. And if you think requiring very young children to close their eyes during a prayer blocks out distractions, then you haven't watched a young child try to keep his or her eyes closed for a period of time. Keeping the eyes closed becomes a distraction in itself. So sometimes it may be more appropriate to keep our eyes open and our heads lifted during a prayer.

Open-eyed prayers are appropriate with young children. They can also be used with all ages, and are particularly effective when thanking God for an item that is before the group. For example, prayers before snack time for young children can be an opportunity for an open-eyed prayer. Look at the snack and ask the children to imagine what it tastes like as you pray. Then, as you continue to look at the snack, thank God for the food.

On a trip to a nearby park with a second-grade class, we used open-eyed prayers. Spring was in its full color, and everywhere the flowers and shrubs seemed to shout praise to God. We used Psalm 96:11-13:

> Be glad, earth and sky!
>   Roar, sea, and every creature in you;
>   be glad, fields, and everything in you!
> The trees in the woods will shout for joy
>   when the Lord comes to rule the earth.
> He will rule the peoples of the world
>   with justice and fairness.

After talking about what we saw before us and how God made the whole world and all that was in it, we each stood in different directions, looking at some specific thing that was beautiful to us, and thanked God in our own minds.

Do We Have to Use Special Words When We Pray?

Children and youth need no special wording in their prayers. We want this to be a natural relationship with God, so we want to use familiar words with them. You can pray to God just as you talk to your friend. Some of the prayers that have been passed down to us from years past have special words because those were the types of words that were used then. But we can use whatever words best express what we want to say to God.

Why Do Some Prayers Use "Thee" and "Thou"?

In formal prayers, the terms "thee," "thou," and "thine" are often used. We no longer use these words in our everyday language, and we may not fully understand them. They are a holdover from the King James Version of the Bible and lend a gentle sound to the prayer. However, we must remember that a prayer is not said for the way it sounds, but rather for the communication between the person praying and God. At the time of the writing of the KJV, there were two sets of pronouns. The words *you* and *yours* were formal, used only for royalty or superiors. The pronouns *thee*, *thou*, and *thine* were used for persons very close to you, such as your family. Therefore using *thee, thou,* and *thine* placed the relationship with God on a very personal level. Over the years we have completely reversed the use of these words.

What Do We Mean When We "Bless" Someone in a Prayer?

Many adults do not understand the meaning of the word *bless*, although we use it often. I can recall thinking as a child that I must be sure to "bless" everyone in my prayers each night, and if I happened to forget one person, I was afraid that some terrible problem would befall that person. This was a hard burden for a seven-year-old to carry, as if I had the responsibility of the fate of those people on my shoulders.

Bless is not a magical word that keeps someone out of harm. Although *bless* and *intercession* are not interchangeable, *bless* might be thought of as loving another person in God. The prayer of intercession releases that person and sets up a channel for God to work.

With young children, perhaps it is more appropriate to express our thanks to God for these people as we pray, instead of using the term "bless." Older elementary children and youth can begin to deal with the concept of blessing another person.

When I Pray "Our Father," Am I Praying to My Daddy?

The word that Jesus used for *father* when he taught the disciples the prayer is actually better translated as "Daddy." Jesus wanted us to feel that God is a personal God, like the most loving parent we could ever know.

It is natural for adults to speak of God as our father or our parent. However, we need to be aware that some children and youth do not have a positive father image in the home, and some do not have a father at all. A child once told a teacher, "My father is mean to me. I can't pray to God as a father, but my mother is kind." The positive concept of God as a parent who is loving and kind is what we want to develop. Consequently, we need to be inclusive in our language about God so that God can be experienced in the loving way that Jesus intended when he said "Our Father."

Do I Pray to Jesus or to God?

When our son was two years old, we had pancakes one morning. His father said, "These are delicious!" My son, Sammie, immediately argued with him that they weren't delicious, but they were pancakes. Young children sometimes have difficulty understanding two definitions for the same word.

There are many ways to address God in a prayer. When we sometimes pray to God and sometimes pray to Jesus, we may give young children mixed signals. The concept of the Trinity is very abstract (see page 32). Adults understand that Jesus was God in an earthly form, and on occasion we may feel more at home praying to Jesus. However, we do not need to use such abstract ideas with young children. They have a lifetime to wrestle and come to grips with abstract theological concepts. It is better to use the term God in our prayers with young children, and help them appreciate Jesus as the person who taught us what God is like. As they grow older, they will better grasp the relationship of the Trinity that we hold so important. As the child's understanding of Jesus grows, it will become natural to pray sometimes to Jesus and sometimes to God.

What Is Sin?

Sin is an act that separates us from God. If an act separates us from God, then it is something that we need to confess in order to right our relationship with God. Often we get hung up on particular "sins" when actually these are only symptoms of the real sin—the real thing that separates us from God. An example of this might be anger. Anger in itself is only a feeling, and neither right nor wrong. However, an attitude that we may have that causes anger, or the way that we express our anger, may be a sin. Perhaps our attitude is a determination to always have our own way; or perhaps we express our anger by hitting another person. These are the things that we need to look at in our confession to God.

We can help children and youth look at why they got "mad" and their responsibility in venting their anger, instead of simply telling them that they must not get mad. The blanket statement "I'm sorry" can become trite if we don't dig deeper into what caused our feelings or why we reacted the way we did.

Why Do We Confess Our Sins?

Confess is a word that children seldom use. In our society, a confession is usually reserved for a major crime. In the religious context, a confession not only admits wrong, but it also brings a determination to change. Children can understand that confession is simply saying "I'm sorry" to God and telling God that you don't want to make the mistake again. This may be a more appropriate way to relate this concept to children.

Why Tell God If God Already Knows Everything?

"But," you say, "God knows that I appreciate the gifts of this earth. God knows that I have done wrong. Why must I thank God, or why must I confess what God already knows?" A good friend is likely to understand that you appreciate his or her kind acts toward you, but when you express it verbally, a closer bond develops between you and your friend. Even if your friend knows you have wronged someone, and you know that the wrong does not threaten your friendship, there will be a strain in your relationship until you openly discuss the wrongdoing with your friend. The strain comes from your own holding back, from your own reservations. The same is true with God. In order to deepen our relationship with God we must be upfront in all we do.

Why Doesn't God Answer My Prayer?

Most teachers have had a student ask this question. It is important to stress that praying is not some magical formula that brings about just what we want. We need to help students realize that prayer is conversation and commitment to God, lining up our lives with God. When we do ask God for specifics, sometimes the answer may be no, but God never allows anything in our lives that we can't handle with God's help. We must realize that when the answer is no, then the "yes" part comes when God gives us the peace to live with the situation. Help students think "Yes, I can make it through this, with God's help." In Philippians 4:13, perhaps we should insert the word *yes* in order to be more affirmative: "*Yes,* I have the strength to face all conditions by the power that Christ gives me."

PRAYER AT HOME

Questions About Prayer Most Often Asked

We all have questions about prayer from time to time. There is no way that we can have all of the answers, and there is no reason for embarrassment in this. Feel free to seek out other adults to discuss any questions that your child may have about prayer. And recognize that their answers may not be the same as yours, and your child may eventually even have different answers from your own. But only through inquiring and doing our own thinking can we develop a personal faith and relationship with God.

Here are some common questions and my own answers. Reflect on these and then decide on your own responses.

Why do we bow our heads and close our eyes when we pray?

It isn't necessary to have specific body positions for prayer, but we sometimes bow our heads as a symbol of recognizing God as special, and we close our eyes to block out distractions.

Do we have to use special words when we pray?

You can pray to God just as you talk to your friend. Sometimes we use special words when we pray together so that we can all pray the same words at the same time.

What do we mean when we "bless" some-one in a prayer?

Bless is not a magical word that keeps some-one out of harm. Bless might be thought of as a way of loving another person in God.

When I pray "Our Father," am I praying to my daddy?

When praying, Jesus used a word in his language that we may translate as "Daddy." By this he meant that God is very much like the most loving parent that we could ever have.

Do I pray to Jesus or to God?

(**Note:** As very young children have difficulty under-standing how their mother can be someone else's sister, they cannot grasp the abstract concept of the Trinity. When we sometimes pray to God and sometimes to Jesus, we give very young children mixed signals. For that age group, it is best to pray to God and reserve the name Jesus as a person who lived long ago and taught us about God. They have a lifetime to grow into the richer meanings of the Trinity.)

We use many names for God, and sometimes we think of Jesus in the same way we think of God.

What is sin?

Sin is acting in a way that keeps us from being close to God.

Why do we confess our sins?

Confession is simply telling God that you are sorry for something you did, and that you don't want to make the mistake again.

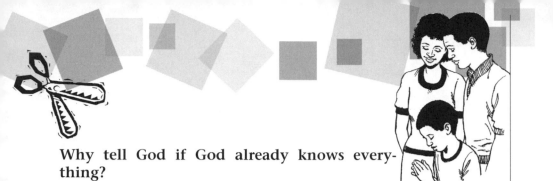

Why tell God if God already knows everything?

You tell a good friend "thank you," even if that person knows you appreciate what he or she has done. You also acknowledge a wrongdoing even if the person knows you've wronged him or her. Telling these things to God makes you feel closer to God.

Why doesn't God answer my prayer?

Praying is not some magical formula to bring us just what we want. Even if the answer is no, God never allows anything in our lives that we can't handle with God's help.

Chapter 3

Age-level Understandings of Prayer

Children and youth vary in their understandings of prayer and in their ability to express themselves to God. It is difficult to say, "You pray with children who are this age in this manner; and if your children are of that age, you pray in that manner." However, there are certain concepts of prayer that young children cannot grasp, even when they feel free to express themselves. There are also some aspects of prayer that we need to consider with all students.

This does not mean that young children cannot worship and pray. In fact, many educators now believe that very young children are dealing with abstract thoughts based on their limited experience.

I recall a two-year-old friend who visited me often in my office at the church. Katy was as comfortable talking to Rainbow, my goldfish, as she was playing in her room at home. One day, as she and her mother were leaving the church after preparing a classroom for Sunday she told her mother, "I know what I want to be when I grow up. I want to be a god!"

Her mother asked, "Do you mean you want to be like Jesus and tell other people about God?"

"No," said Katy. "I want to be a god!"

Wisely, her mother asked, "Why do you want to be a god?"

Katy replied, "I want to be a god, because God loves everybody, and I want to love everybody."

At age two, Katy was dealing with real theological concepts in the best way she knew how. She could not label the concept as the grace of God, but nonetheless she experienced the concept and was grasping for its meaning.

Each child deals with abstract thinking differently. Some children will develop an abstract thought process earlier than others. That thought process does not appear overnight, in full bloom, but comes about slowly. As children gain more experience on which to base their thinking, and as their communication skills develop, they can relate to and communicate more abstract concepts. This process usually isn't complete until middle to high school age.

Even as adults, we often grapple with many abstract concepts, and so it is no surprise that children have difficulty dealing with some of our theological concepts such as the Trinity, eternity, and salvation. Children can repeat the definition of these terms that we have taught them, but often this is only lip service. They are working with their own experiences as they develop abstract thinking, and those experiences are limited. When it is difficult for children to understand that their mother is also the daughter of their grandmother, we cannot expect them to understand our God as three persons. Since they cannot understand the finality of our earthly death, they have no way to relate a real understanding of what eternity means. Until they develop attitudes and values, they have no background for understanding salvation. Remember that young children are dealing with their own experiences, not ours. We must begin where they are.

Formal Prayers

Older elementary children and youth can learn some of the special prayers of the church. With this age group you can begin talking about the different parts of such prayers and experiment with developing prayers that contain these parts. The ACTS of prayer that was discussed in chapter 1 is a good way to look at formal prayers.

Elementary children can begin wording prayers in a more formal way. These might be used in the congregational worship from time to time. This gives the children an appreciation of their participation in the worship experience. It is important that the words of all unison prayers in worship be printed in the bulletin or have a page reference so that they can be located in a hymnal or worship book. Not only do children and youth benefit from this, but it also is a welcoming gesture for those who are new to congregational worship.

As some of us were growing up we learned the words of the Lord's Prayer in the school classroom. Since this no longer occurs in public schools, it is important that we help children learn the prayer at home and in the church. Young children cannot understand many of the words. However, once a child takes part in congregational worship, it is important for him or her to begin to learn the words. It will help the child feel a part of the total church family by praying the prayer along with the rest of the congregation.

Dick Murray, a former professor of Christian education at Perkins School of Theology, said it is important for children to learn the words of the Lord's Prayer and familiar responses sung in worship by age three. They will not understand the words, but they will know it is an important thing that belongs to them. Murray once told the story of his three-year-old grandson. He often took his grandson with him when he was driving in Dallas. They would sing the Gloria Patri together in the car, with the grandson sitting in his car seat singing, "Glory PawPaw; glory PawPaw." One Sunday when they were worshiping together and everyone stood to sing the response together, the grandson tugged on Murray's jacket and said with joy, "PawPaw, they're singing our song!"

Youth may also need help with the meaning. We will cover the Lord's Prayer in more detail on page 55. The guidelines listed below will help as you work with your children and youth in prayer. The following chapters will give you concrete suggestions for ways to move them into a personal relationship with God through prayer.

Age-level Understandings

YOUNGER PRESCHOOL

▶Associate prayer with good things.
▶Pray prayers of thanksgiving and praise.
▶Pray with the child as if you are talking to God. Begin the relationship with God.
▶Use simple language: you and your, not thee, thou, and thine (see page 23).
▶Learn simple singing prayers.
▶No particular body position is necessary.
▶A child need not always close his or her eyes.
▶Giving thanks for food after eating makes more sense to this age child.

OLDER PRESCHOOL

▶Pray spontaneous prayers. "Talk" to God.
▶Prayer can be two to five short sentences of everyday speech. Pray with words the child understands.
▶Provide opportunities for a child to add something to prayers.
▶Prayer is not a time to show off. Be cautious of asking a young child to pray before guests unless you know he or she is very comfortable with it.
▶Evening prayers: Talk over happy times of the day, kindnesses, how God helped; then pray.
▶Begin requests for help: "Help me to remember to cross the street carefully . . . to take turns . . . to help others."
▶Pray for someone else: "Help the doctor to help Johnny."
▶Begin to distinguish between asking Daddy for toys and asking God to help us take turns. God works through people for physical needs.
▶Begin learning the Lord's Prayer (see page 55) and responses sung in worship.

KINDERGARTEN–GRADES 1-2

▶Continue praise and thanksgiving.
▶Let the child compose his or her own written prayers.
▶Create litany prayers together (see page 91).
▶Give opportunities for sentence prayers after discussion of what we are thankful for; don't force the child to pray. Acknowledge need for forgiveness.
▶Encourage prayers asking for help, making them more specific than before.
▶Learn the Lord's Prayer (see page 55) and responses sung in worship.
▶Begin to provide some personal devotional materials such as *Pockets*, a devotional magazine for children (see Discipleship Resources at www.discipleshipresources.org; or call 800-925-6847 or 800-972-0433).

GRADES 3-5

▶Encourage personal and private worship. Provide devotional material. An excellent source for this is *Pockets*, a devotional magazine for children (see Discipleship Resources at www.discipleshipresources.org).
▶Study prayers in the hymnal for special occasions.
▶Help the child appreciate the prayers in formal worship.
▶Introduce journaling prayers (see page 81).
▶Continue to talk about prayer as a close relationship with God.
▶Encourage growth so that this relationship with God is there when the child is more independent.

MIDDLE AND HIGH SCHOOLERS

▶Continue to encourage personal and private worship.
▶Expand use of formal prayers and learn about the authors.
▶Provide time and materials for regular journaling in the classroom and at home (see page 81).
▶Include intercessory prayers.
▶Prayers for guidance will help youth over difficult times.

PRAYER AT HOME
Age-level
Understandings of Prayer

We are discovering that young children have experiences of worship in some form, even when they do not verbalize them. Their prayers may even be expressed as conversations with a favorite doll or a pet. Their base for understanding just does not allow them to express these experiences as prayers.

Young children cannot understand some of the abstract concepts that we often use in prayers, but it is important for them to feel a part of the church family. Consequently, it is good to teach all children some of those prayers that we use when the church family worships together, even if the concepts are beyond them. Find opportunities as a family to learn any prayers that you use in worship at church. Talk through the words that they can understand and explain that many of these prayers were written long ago and have been prayed by Christians for many years.

Look through your hymnal and be aware of songs and hymns that you sing in worship that can also be used as prayers. You might read or sing some of them at mealtime and bedtime, or even when you are driving in the automobile.

As children grow and mature in their concepts, they can become more comfortable with some of the formal forms of prayer. However, if your child is older and you are just introducing prayer, begin with very simple methods. One of the simplest is to talk over events of the day or things that we are thankful for before a prayer. Then you can simply pray, "Thank you God for all these things that we have talked about." The actual praying happens during the discussion, and the spoken prayer merely affirms it.

It is important to spontaneously pray with your children. Thank God for various gifts and experiences in your life, for opportunities to care for others, and for persons whom you meet.

The attached list will help you work with your child, no matter what the age.

Attachment:
Age-level Understandings

Chapter 4

Prayer and Our Intelligences and Personalities

The style of prayer used to talk to God will vary because it depends on the content of your prayer, the age of those with whom you are praying, each person's personality, and even each person's favored way of learning. We are discovering that different people come to prayer in different ways. A style of prayer that is meaningful to me may not be meaningful to you. And a class, or even a family, may have persons with varying ways of praying.

I have already discussed the approach to use when praying with various age levels. In this chapter I will deal with *multiple intelligences* and the part that personality plays in our spiritual prayer life.

Audio and Visual

I have encouraged praying with open eyes ever since my college days when I learned about the characteristics of young children. However, it was not until recently that I recognized just why I appreciate the permission to pray with my eyes open. I discovered that I am a far more visual person than someone with an audio preference. An example of this is when a high-energy worship service is planned and led by folks with an audio-learning preference, and they neglect to include something for us visual folks. A focal point helps me center my worship and my prayer. I love and appreciate music, but without some focal point, the music does not seem to move me.

Any time I lead a worship experience, teach a class, or even preside at a business meeting, I make sure there is some focal point for those who are visually oriented. Most often I include a candle because it is a good reminder that Christ is among us in our gathering. With that visual reminder, we can be much more conscious of God's presence.

Many families are developing worship or prayer centers in their homes. I find that my best place for prayer is on my porch or some other location where I can look at God's world. Each classroom should have a worship or celebration center where the class can gather for a time of prayer; then when the elements in the center are changed to correspond to the subject of study, it will have more meaning.

Multiple Intelligences

Recent research has revealed multiple ways that people learn. These ways of learning, or *multiple intelligences,* can also be applied to our prayer life. Howard Gardner, an authority on brain research, identified several intelligences that God gave each of us. We all use these intelligences, but each person favors one or two more than the others.

- *Verbal/Linguistic* refers to language and words, both written and spoken. *Jesus approached his listeners in this manner with his stories.*

- *Logical/Mathematical* includes inductive thinking and reasoning, statistics, and abstract patterns. *Jesus used questions and answers to reach his listeners who learned in this way.*

- *Visual/Spatial* deals with visualizing objects and creating mental pictures. *Jesus used common objects to explain his meaning to persons who learn in this manner.*

- *Body/Kinesthetic* relates to the physical, such as movement and physical activity. *Jesus involved the disciples in learning through fishing and washing their feet.*

- *Musical/Rhythmic* involves recognition of patterns, both tonal and rhythmic. *Singing hymns was a part of the common experience of Jesus and his disciples.*

- *Interpersonal* follows relationships between persons, including true communication. *Jesus worked with persons on a personal level and also developed small groups, his most successful group being the twelve disciples.*

- *Intrapersonal* denotes self-reflection and awareness of that within us that guides us. *Many times the Bible men-*

tions *Jesus drawing away from others for solitude (by himself or with his disciples) or for reflection.*

- **Nature** denotes learning through nature. *Jesus used nature in many of his illustrations. He taught outdoors most of the time.*[1]

Spiritual Personalities

Prayer is the heart of our spirituality. Without prayer we are hollow with false fronts of spirituality. Therefore it is important to recognize how your personality, and the personality of those whom we teach to pray, fits with spirituality.

In his book *Knowing Me, Knowing God*, Malcolm Goldsmith uses the Myers-Briggs personality test to explore spirituality. He includes a questionnaire that helps individuals examine the relationship of their personality and spirituality.

Spiritual Personality Summary[2]

Sensing spirituality persons
- take in information through their senses.
- music, speaking, and silence are important to them, as are touch, and smell, and taste.
- concerned with specifics and with the "here and now," what is happening today in the circumstances of life rather than vague, generalized plans about the future.
- want to cut out words and ideas and see spirituality in the simplest form.
- "Don't talk about it, show me!"

iNtuitive spirituality persons
- take in information through their imagination.
- future-oriented, aware of possibilities, living in a provisional world, looking and hoping for a new and better situation.
- concerned with the "big picture" rather than details.

1. List taken from Delia Halverson, *Nuts & Bolts of Christian Education* (Nashville: Abingdon Press, 2000), p. 10.
2. The following excerpt is from Halverson, *Nuts & Bolts of Christian Education,* pp. 60-61.

- quickly become bored with repetition, practicalities, and the minutiae of plans and present circumstances.
- attracted to a theology that places stress on the reign of God bringing about justice and peace.
- God is so mysterious and wonderful that words to describe God become meaningless.
- receive as much insight into the workings of God by reading novels as they do from reading the Bible.
- scripture is likely to be used as a launching-off point for reflective thought about issues, expecting that God will use that Bible passage to bring other things to mind.

Feeling spirituality persons
- think that decisions are good if they take other people into account, and they will put themselves out for the sake of others.
- place themselves in other people's shoes and enjoy helping others.
- prize peace and harmony and go to considerable lengths to create such conditions, often at personal expense or inconvenience.
- often turn a blind eye to things which ought to be challenged or to people who need to be confronted.
- identify with gospel images and situations: sacrificial victim, turning the other cheek, going the extra mile, and bearing the suffering of others. It is almost as though it is more Christlike to be hurt.
- sometimes an unconscious desire to be exploited or "put upon," interpreted as a sign of authentic discipleship.
- commitment to a church community is important, getting to know people in order to discover their needs and troubles and provide strength.

Thinking spirituality persons
("Thinking" in a technical sense, not to imply that those who prefer the Feeling function are non-thinkers)

- God perceived as being primarily righteous, just, faithful, true, consistent, wise, and reasonable (not offending reason).
- truth is truth and cannot be molded or twisted to suit circumstances or to avoid giving offense.
- firm, logical, cool, and analytical spirituality.
- can be assertive, critical, adversarial, distant, and impersonal.
- stewards of creation, responsible and concerned about truth and justice.
- God makes demands on our lives, requiring us to live with integrity and to seek righteousness and freedom.
- like objectivity and exactness.
- like public worship to be done decently and with order.
- tend not to like their privacy being invaded, especially if they are also introverts.
- the very process of thinking can be a form of spiritual exercise and an offering to God.
- may question prayers and hymns, checking out their words to see if they are logical, consistent, or true.

PRAYER AT HOME

Prayer and Our Intelligences and Personalities

Recent research indicates that the way we grow in our spirituality often depends on certain personalities and preferences for learning.

Audio and Visual

Audio and visual stimulus enhance everyone in their prayer life. However, persons who operate best through the visual need focal points to help them center their worship and prayer. Persons who prefer audio need more verbal and musical experiences in worship and prayer. Many families are developing worship or prayer centers in their homes. Be sure to include opportunities for both audio and visual stimulus in your home, and keep the prayer experiences fresh by changing these frequently.

Multiple Intelligences

Howard Gardner, an authority on brain research, identified several intelligences that God gave each of us. These intelligences may be used to help us develop our prayer life. We operate out of all of these intelligences, but some of us favor certain ones. As you learn which intelligences are favored by your children, you will be better able to assist them in their prayer life. Look over the attached listing of intelligences and identify those that are dominant to your child.

Spiritual Personalities

Just as we learn through various intelligences, much of our spiritual growth depends on our personalities. Some of us find high-energy worship to be most meaningful. Some worship best with the rich tradition of liturgy and symbols of the church. Others search for opportunities to worship in a contemplative or reflective mode. It is important to offer your children various forms of worship and prayer, and to encourage them to search for those means of reaching God that are most significant to them. The attached spiritual personality summary will help your own growth as well as help you know how to help your children with their prayer lives.

Attachments:
Multiple Intelligences
Spiritual Personality Summary

Chapter 5

Memorized Prayers

We often hear amusing stories of children's interpretations of memorized prayers. A Christian education colleague told me the story of her niece's version of the Lord's Prayer. Her niece began, "Our Father, who aren't in heaven, how do you know my name?" An adult may consider such an incident cute or amusing. But if we look more closely at this child's interpretation, we see that she was reaching out to God with a need that God be personal enough to know her name. Even memorized prayers need to be personal, because prayer is a very personal communication between individuals and God.

Left Brain/Right Brain

In Matthew 22:37 Jesus gave the Pharisee the greatest commandment, "Love the Lord your God with all your heart, with all your soul, and with all your mind." Jesus recognized the importance of using all of our mind, and I believe this is necessary in our prayer life as well as in our study.

In recent years much has been published about the functions of the left and right sides of our brain. Scientists believe that the left side of our brain is used for rational and analytical thinking. This is the side that memorizes well. The symbolic, intuitive, meditative, and visual facets of our prayer life are handled by the right side of our brain. In order to have a healthy prayer life, it is important that we learn to function with both sides of our brain.

Some of us are more adept at using one side of our brain than the other. Memorization comes quite easy for some, but is more challenging for others. It is important that no child or youth feel that he or she is inadequate because memorization is difficult.

I spoke with a teacher who used rewards for memorization, and shared with her my personal difficulty with memorization. I didn't learn the alphabet until I was in the third grade, and I have memorized the books of the Bible three times but cannot recite them even now. When I was a child, other students were able to memorize easily while I would practice and practice, only to reverse a phrase or substitute a synonym. The teacher responded in surprise, "Why, I have always had such ease with memorization that I thought when a student didn't memorize something, it was only because of lack of study." Many teachers assume everyone likes to memorize. Memorization comes from repeated use of something, or when something becomes memorable. Memorization for memorization's sake is often not lasting, and motivation for such is hard to come by for most students.

You will also find that although some children and youth memorize easily, they have difficulty verbalizing their thoughts in prayer. This may be particularly true with older children and youth who have never prayed in public. By using the suggestions in the next two chapters, you can help these young people feel more confident.

We need to have a balance of both left- and right-brain types of prayer. Be aware of different students' specific needs. Since prayer is a personal and private experience, even when shared aloud, show understanding for those you are leading to prayer.

Whether you are using memorized or spontaneous prayer, always give children and youth the option of public participation in prayer. Rather than "going around the circle" in prayer, instead begin a prayer time yourself and close it with a memorized or singing prayer that everyone knows or is learning. Suggest that anyone who would like to should feel free to offer a prayer in between.

Memorization Aids

To really pray a memorized prayer, we must understand the words. Use awareness of age understandings when choosing prayers, and, for children who still think concretely, avoid selecting prayers with abstract meanings. Go through the prayer and explain in simple language any unfamiliar words. If you memorize prayers from our Christian heritage that use *thee* or *thou,* explain that the words were used a long time ago in the place of our word *you.* Older children and youth may be interested in the information on page 23 that relates to these terms.

- Children who read can use a **card game** to understand the meaning of words in a memorized prayer. Write all of the words or phrases of the prayer on cards. On the back of any card with a word or phrase that is unfamiliar, write the definition in a different color. Using a copy of the prayer, ask a student to arrange the word/phrase cards in order. Any words that are new or unfamiliar may then be turned over to display the definition. The prayer may be read using the definition side of the cards first. Then turn the definition cards back over and practice the prayer.
- Create an **audiotape** with a prayer to be memorized. These tapes are not only useful in a group setting, but are also great for families to use in the car while traveling. They may even be used during a family devotion or at an evening prayer time.
- A **pocket board** is a great help because students can see the words as they memorize the prayer. A pocket board is made by taking a poster board and creating long pockets across the board with folded strips of long paper:

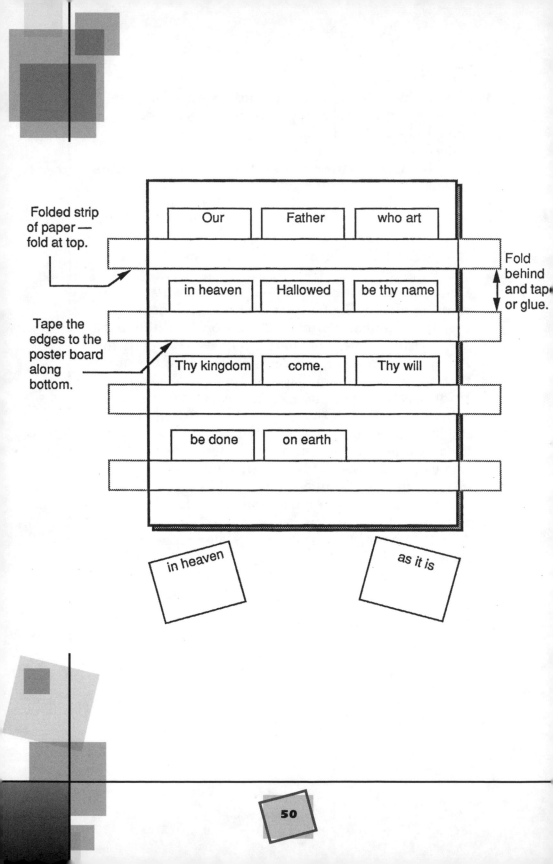

Folded strip of paper — fold at top.

Our | Father | who art

Fold behind and tape or glue.

in heaven | Hallowed | be thy name

Tape the edges to the poster board along bottom.

Thy kingdom | come. | Thy will

be done | on earth

in heaven

as it is

Use these directions for making a pocket board:

Materials needed:
- ❏▸ 1 piece of poster board or heavy cardboard (22 by 28 inches)
- ❏▸ 2 three-inch strips of paper (may use freezer or shelf paper), each thirty inches long
- ❏▸ Transparent tape
- ❏▸ Index cards (same number as there are words or phrases)

Procedure:

Fold the long strips of paper in half lengthwise. Placing the fold at the top, space evenly down the poster board (see illustration), taping them across the bottom and folding the ends around the edges of the poster board, taping them to secure.

Write words or phrases of the prayer at the top of three-by-five-inch cards, and place them in order in the pockets. Read the prayer together several times, using all of the cards. Then each time you read the prayer, randomly remove one of the cards. Soon you will be saying the prayer without the cards.

You can also create the same learning experience by simply placing the cards face-up on the floor or a table and removing cards as you learn the prayer.

Psalm Prayers

The book of Psalms is actually a book of songs and prayers. There are verses from many psalms that are appropriate for young children to learn, and whole sections that older children and youth can learn. The psalms were composed by different people over a long period of time and came to be a part of the Hebrew life and later an important part of the early church.

Some of the prayers in the book portray the personal feelings of an individual, and others are prayers that express the feelings of a group. There are prayers of praise and thanksgiving, and prayers for God's blessing. There are also ones for help, forgiveness, protection, and salvation.

Many of the psalms are quoted in the New Testament, and Jesus frequently used them. From the early beginnings, they have always been a part of the Christian church, and we often use them in worship today.

Be aware of different translations of psalms as you consider memorized prayers. If it is one that is frequently used in worship, you may want to learn the version that is used by your church. Some of us learned passages from the King James Version of the Bible, which is sprinkled with *thee* and *thou*. As suggested on page 23, these words do not feel as natural to children and youth as they do to us. Since we want to help them feel at ease in talking with God, consider other translations. The Good News Translation (formerly known as Today's English Version and Good News Bible) and the Contemporary English Version present Psalms in a very personal way. Compare the following translations of Psalm 104:1*a*, 10-12:

Contemporary English Version	Good News Translation	King James Version
I praise you, LORD God, with all my heart. You are glorious and majestic. . . . You provide streams of water in the hills and valleys, so that the donkeys and other wild animals can satisfy their thirst. Birds build their nests nearby and sing in the trees.	O LORD, my God, how great you are! . . . You make springs flow in the valleys, and rivers run between the hills. They provide water for the wild animals; there the wild donkeys quench their thirst. In the trees near by, the birds make their nests and sing.	Bless the LORD, O my soul. O LORD my God, thou art very great. . . . He sendeth the springs into the valleys, which run among the hills. They give drink to every beast of the field: the wild asses quench their thirst. By them shall the fowls of the heaven have their habitation, which sing among the branches.

Youth will enjoy and benefit from comparing the use of language in a variety of translations and paraphrases.

Because the ancient Hebrew poetry did not have rhyme and meter as we know it, most of the translations are free verse. However, there is a parallelism that most translations have preserved. A statement is made at the beginning of the psalm, then repeated—sometimes in the exact words and sometimes in a modified fashion—throughout the psalm.

Below I have suggested several ways to involve your students in the psalms. The activity suggestions in the remaining chapters can also be adapted easily to the psalms.

Activities Using Psalms

1. Children and youth can pray psalms in a more personal way by substituting their own name at places where a personal pronoun is used.

2. Read the psalm in various translations and discuss ways they vary in wording. Then ask which words make the psalm more meaningful to us today and why.

3. Create a group litany, using passages of praise from the psalms as the group response (see page 91).

4. Using the suggestions under poetry prayers on page 77, create your own prayer psalms as individuals or as a group.

The following are examples of some appropriate psalm passages for children. These may be read as their own prayers or memorized. Consider using passages from the Good News Translation or Contemporary English Version of the Bible.

The Lord's Prayer

Children develop their faith primarily through experiences and relationships. Therefore it is of prime impor-

Psalm Prayers for Young Children

Psalm 8:1*a*	Psalm 30:12*b*	Psalm 104:1*a*
Psalm 9:1	Psalm 41:13	Psalm 118:28*a*
Psalm 9:2	Psalm 75:1*a*	

Psalm Prayers for Older Children

Psalm 5:1-3	Psalm 38:21-22	Psalm 63:1-5
Psalm 8	Psalm 51:1-2	Psalm 86:8-10
Psalm 9:1-2	Psalm 51:10	Psalm 90:1-2
Psalm 16:11	Psalm 51:15	Psalm 108:3-5
Psalm 19:14	Psalm 57:9-10	Psalm 119:89-91
Psalm 36:5-7	Psalm 61:1-3	Psalm 139:1-4

Psalm Prayers for Youth

Most of the psalms are appropriate for youth. Here are a few you might use for special times:

Morning prayer	Psalm 5
Prayer in troubled times	Psalm 6
Complaint about evil people	Psalm 10
Prayer for guidance	Psalm 25
Prayer to be near God	Psalm 42
Prayer for forgiveness	Psalm 51
Prayer of lament for safety	Psalm 142
Prayer of praise	Psalm 145

tance for them to feel a part of worship services and group experiences in the church.

The words of the Lord's Prayer make it primarily an adult prayer. However, as the central prayer that Christians everywhere use, it is important for children to begin to learn it as soon as they are a part of a congregation or other group using the prayer. Many of the words may be beyond their understanding, but the opportunity to "belong" far outweighs the problems of not grasping the words.

Young children need to know that this is a prayer that Jesus taught us to pray, and one that Christians all over the world use. Words can be explained in simple terms, using some of the ideas listed below for elementary children. The wording of the prayer on page 56 is from the Revised Standard Version of the Bible.

In most translations of the Bible, this is where Matthew's direct quotation from Jesus ends. However, as early as the end of the third century, people were using this prayer in their worship services, and they found such joy over the words of the prayer that they just continued the prayer, using some of the words from 1 Chronicles 29:10-13. The following words have been added by tradition and are commonly used with the passage from Matthew 6.

For Thine is the kingdom, and the power, and the glory	*The close of the prayer again says that we believe that God is over all the world and universe (kingdom), and is the greatest.*
Forever.	*We know that God is forever, with no end.*
Amen.	*The word* amen *means "I agree" or "may it be so."*

Our Father	Because God is like a good father, Jesus used the word *Father*. By using the word *our* we realize that God loves all of us and wants us to work together.
who art in heaven,	The word *art* is an old way of saying "is." When we speak of God being in heaven, it does not mean far away, but rather that God is everywhere and is greater than we can understand.
Hallowed be thy name.	*Hallowed* is a way of praising God; it is another word for *holy, awe,* or *wonder.*
Thy kingdom come, **Thy will be done,** **On earth as it is in heaven.**	With these words we pray that all of us on earth will live as God wants, loving one another.
Give us this day our daily bread;	When we pray for "our daily bread," we realize that God made the world that produces food for us to eat. Food is also a part of God's plan, and God is dependable. We also realize that all of our daily needs are important to God. Notice that Jesus did not use *"my* daily bread," but *"our."* The prayer doesn't ask for everything we want each day, but for what we need.
And forgive us our debts,	We recognize that we all sin. *Debt* is a very old word for sin. Sometimes we use the word *trespass*, which in this context is another word for sin. The real meaning for sin is that we "separate ourselves from God." When we sin, we do something or think something that keeps us from being close to God. We ask God to forgive us, knowing that we are forgiven if we are truly sorry.
As we also have forgiven our debtors	We also tell God that we forgive others of sins against us. We realize that we must forgive in order to set ourselves right with God.
And lead us not into temptation,	A temptation is when we want to do something other than what God wants us to do.
But deliver us from evil.	We realize that God's help is available for us and that we will need it to follow God's good plan for us.

Elementary children, and youth can read the prayer from the Bible. When you study the prayer, look at several Bible translations. Remind students that the New Testament was first written in Greek, and that we have different versions because some Greek words do not have exact words that mean the same thing in English. Explain that the wording we use for The Lord's Prayer has traveled through many generations of believers, although we find the original form in Matthew 6:9-13. Luke carries a shorter version of the prayer in verses 2-4 of chapter 11.

We call this The Lord's Prayer because Jesus taught it to his disciples, and we often call Jesus Lord. Through the years the prayer has been translated into many different languages, and is now prayed all over the world. Sometimes the wording varies a little. For example, in English, some churches use *debts,* and others *trespasses.* When Scripture is translated into other languages, the closest word in meaning to the original is substituted. No matter what the language, this magnificent prayer is prayed by Christians everywhere.

Historic Prayers

In our early church heritage and through the years, many people composed meaningful prayers, some of which we use to this day when we pray together. Older children and youth can grasp the time element in history. It is important for them to be exposed to some of the prayers of our Christian heritage. Preface memorization of these prayers by using an experiential learning process, such as paraphrasing the words or drawing illustrations of the prayer.

Using your church hymnal or other worship sources, locate prayers that are used regularly in your services. These prayers, both sung and spoken, may be used as calls to worship, prayers of confession, offertory prayers, and benedictions. Learning them will help students participate in worship. Look at the prayers in the ritual of your communion service. Discuss the meanings of the words and pray the prayers together often so that the students will be familiar with them and can later participate fully in the service. Many of these prayers use *thee* and *thou;* you will want to use the information on page 23 to explain their usage. If you are teaching a class, be aware of sporadic attendance that results in a student not having been in class when you explained the words before.

Art is another excellent way of introducing historic prayers. By illustrating them, you look at the meaning of the words and life situations relating to the prayer. Help children and youth appreciate the prayers that are used in your worship services through art. You may want to consider making banners or posters that can be used in the sanctuary for a period of time.

Heritage Prayers

Historic prayers are embedded in our church liturgy. I have identified heritage prayers as being those from Christians in the past, but not usually a part of our established liturgy. The following are examples of heritage prayers:

> Thou hast made us for thyself, and our heart is restless, until it finds rest in thee.
>
> (St. Augustine, 354–450)

> Christ with me, Christ before me, Christ behind me, Christ in me, Christ beneath me, Christ above me, Christ on my right, Christ on my left,
> Christ where I lie, Christ where I sit, Christ where I arise, Christ in the heart of every one who thinks of me, Christ in the mouth of every one who speaks to me, Christ in every eye that sees me, Christ in every ear that hears me. Salvation is of the Lord, Salvation is of the Christ. May your salvation, O Lord, be ever with us.
>
> (St. Patrick, 389–461)

May the road rise to meet you. May the wind be always at your back. May the sun shine warm upon your face. May the rains fall softly upon your fields until we meet again. May God hold you in the hollow of his hand.

(Old Gaelic blessing)

O Lord our God, grant us grace to desire thee with our whole heart; that so desiring, we may seek and find thee; and so finding thee, we may love thee; and loving thee, we may hate those sins from which thou hast redeemed us; for the sake of Jesus Christ.

(St. Anselm, 1033–1109)

Lord, make me according to thy heart.

(Brother Lawrence, 1611–1691)

God be in my head, and in my understanding; God be in my eyes, and in my looking; God be in my mouth, and in my speaking; God be in my heart, and in my thinking; God be at my end, and at my departing.

(Old Sarum Primer)

Thou art never weary, O Lord, of doing us good. Let us never be weary of doing thee service. But, as thou hast pleasure in the prosperity of thy servants, so let us take pleasure in the service of our Lord, and abound in thy work, and in thy love and praise evermore. O fill up all that is wanting, reform whatever is amiss in us, perfect the thing that concerneth us. Let the witness of thy pardoning love ever abide in all our hearts.

(John Wesley, 1703–1791)

Drop thy still dews of quietness,
Till all our strivings cease;
Take from our souls the strain and stress,
And let our ordered lives confess
The beauty of thy peace.

(J. G. Whittier, 1807–1892)

Chapter 6

Spontaneous Prayer

It was Sunday morning, and the teacher and preschoolers were on their hands and knees, centering their attention on the floor. Before them marched a parade of ants carefully moving crumbs of an abandoned cookie from the table to their home somewhere outside. The teacher said, "Look at those tiny legs. God made the tiny ants and made them with such strength that they can carry crumbs bigger than they are. I thank you, God, for the chance to see your ants today."[1]

To persons passing in the hall, the scene may have appeared strange. But to the teacher and children, this was an experience in spontaneous prayer. Experiential opportunities are important for children's faith journey. Indeed, such opportunities are important for all of us. Spontaneous prayer brings God out of the "there and then" and into the "here and now," helping children and youth relate God to their own lives.

Spontaneous prayers are appropriate for all of us, whether we are young children or adults. We do not need to wait for a formal prayer time to thank God for a beautiful sunset or for an act of kindness from a friend. Whether you work with children or youth, there are times when spontaneous prayer can be a natural part of our living and learning together.

Talking prayers work best in spontaneous situations. There's no need for some formal type of prayer, just simply talk with God. Depending on the situation, you may sometimes choose to keep your eyes open, smiling into one another's faces or looking at the object about which you are praying.

Begin spontaneous prayer by talking about what you see or what you experience. As you work with prayer, you will become alert to opportunities to pray spontaneously. You will also learn to weave such occasions into your curriculum or your planned activity as a family. What follows are examples of ways to incorporate spontaneous prayer into the life you share.

As You Eat Together

Take advantage of occasions when you share food together. Singing or memorized prayers are appropriate at snack times. Consider some of the suggestions on page 121. In the classroom, be aware that some parents may have strict rules about singing at the table. Assure the children that singing a prayer is different from singing and disturbing others. Help them understand that singing prayers is a way of praising God.

Vary your prayer experiences. Sometimes you may want to thank God before you eat, and sometimes it is good to thank God after you have eaten, remembering how good it tasted. Try varying the prayer throughout the year. If you teach very young children, and you plan to pray before eating, it may be wise to leave the snacks visible but not hand them out individually until after the prayer.

In Nature

As you teach find opportunities to share God's creation and experience spontaneous prayer. Be aware of what is happening in nature, and talk about it, including prayers of thanksgiving in your conversation. Using suggestions from other chapters in this book, help the children and youth compose prayers about God's creation. Of course you will need to be aware of the comprehension and understanding abilities of the specific age levels. Young children can understand simple thank-you prayers for items in God's creation. Older children and youth can begin to grasp the miracles of the workings of God in the world.

After a rain, thank God for providing water for us and for all living things. Then talk about the importance of water. When you experience an electrical storm, older children and youth can thank God for giving us electricity. The class might think of all the things that we would not have if God had not made electricity, or if persons before us had not used the brains that God gave them to learn how to use electricity.

As seasons change, talk with the students about the dependability of God that is shown through the seasons. Day following night, sprouting bulbs, the movement of the stars, and the tides are also signs of the dependability of God. Offer a thank-you prayer for such a dependable God. Youth and adults become more appreciative of God's seasons when we speak openly of them.

Develop a nature table and place on it items from God's creation for which we are thankful. This is appropriate not only for preschoolers who love show-and-tell, but also for elementary students. Consider placing an encyclopedia or science reference book on the table for doing research. As you have a worship or conversation time, encourage children to talk about what they brought for the table. After those who brought something, and those who have researched it have shared, you can offer a prayer of thanks for everything, or you may create a litany using the suggestions on page 91.

Planning Projects

Service projects may be as simple as making a thank-you card for a custodian, or a get-well card for a classmate, or as involved as planning a parent/child project whereby you help to clean up or paint a senior's home in the neighborhood. Elementary children and youth have the ability to think of their projects as ministry and see their work as an outreach of the church.

All children and youth can see such experiences as ways to share what they have learned with others. They can also understand that doing things for others, caring for them, and showing them love are done because Jesus taught us to live this way. In this way we show that we love Jesus.

As you plan service projects with your class, take time to ask for God's guidance before you make a decision about what you will do. The prayer may vary, depending on the ages of those involved. With younger children, a simple prayer will be appropriate, such as, "God, we want to help _____. We ask you to be with us as we make plans to help. Amen."

As experience with prayer deepens you may lengthen the prayer to summarize the different choices that you have before you, then ask for guidance. After deciding, ask God to be with you as you begin your ministry with whomever you are working.

Thanksgiving Prayers

Prayers of thanksgiving are appropriate for all ages and at any time of the year. When you include them in your daily life, they become *thanksliving* prayers. Be alert to the times in your curriculum or in your everyday life when you can naturally include a prayer of thanksgiving. For example, there will be times when you consider the workers of the church or other helpers in the community or at home, or when you consider mission projects that the church does, or when you thank God for those in our past heritage who have contributed to our church or family. These can be natural times to offer prayers of thanks.

Thanksgiving prayers are appropriate during a celebration. Whenever it seems appropriate, stop for a moment for prayer. Sometimes a simple "Thank you, God, for such good times together" expresses the feelings of appreciation to God.

Don't forget to talk about the children's and youth's own gifts from God, their talents and abilities. Help them to see that God's gifts are not limited to musical or artistic talents. Assure them that an ability to listen to someone else's problem and let the person know that you care is a gift or talent from God. If a child has an ability to understand math, or if a child can make up a good story, recognize these as gifts from God and offer thanks for them.

Personal Relationships

Be aware of relationships. Young children often have difficulty sharing toys and need help in learning this art. Older children also have difficulties with relationships. Youth focus their lives on relationships. Pray for broken relationships. When they have been restored, you may want to pray a simple prayer of thanks with those involved. Unless this has blown out of proportion and involves the whole class, keep these prayers private and between the persons involved.

Older preschool and elementary children can begin to use prayers of confession. It may be appropriate to suggest that they silently offer a prayer, telling God that they are sorry for whatever caused their broken relationship. Then you may close with a sentence, thanking God for the healed relationship. First Peter 3:8a may be appropriate here: "Finally, all of you, live in harmony with one another" (NIV). Share the verse by simply stating that you are happy they are learning to live together as the Bible tells us to do, then say the verse.

Developing Spontaneous Prayers

Periodically, tell children or youth that you thank God you were able to all be together. Do this in spontaneous conversation and individually, rather than as a ritual. Encourage prayers to develop in a spontaneous way, taking prayer out of a routine context. In this way, children and youth learn to turn to God any time and in all circumstances instead of just at mealtimes or bedtimes. Consider introducing them to the "Breath Prayer" found on pages 75-76.

Be aware that your spontaneous prayers become a model. As children and youth become more at ease with your praying naturally, they will begin to see opportunities to do so themselves. Their personal, spontaneous prayers may come about through their inner thoughts, and you may never hear them spoken aloud. However, be aware that you are laying the groundwork for that personal relationship between God and the student.

In the Classroom

- As the children or youth arrive, greet each one individually. By using names, you let them know that you think they are important. Talk about how you thank God that he or she is present, that you are thankful it is Sunday, and that you can all be together in the class.
- If you experienced something beautiful on the way to church, you might talk about it and say that you thank God for it. As your class feels more comfortable with spontaneous prayer, encourage the children and youth to share their own experiences.
- Activities during a class need to be a part of the whole learning process. Most curriculum writers suggest activities that give experiences related to the purpose of the session. Be conscious of how your activities give the students experiences in faith, and look for opportunities to pray spontaneously about those experiences. If you prepare gifts for other people, thank God for the opportunity to share love with others. If you make some object that visually expands the purpose of the ses-

sion, comment on the student's work and thank God for it. For younger children, acknowledge how much more capable they are of such work (that is, cutting, pasting, drawing, and so forth) than they were some months ago. Thank God for this growth.

- As preschoolers play you should move around the room, listening to the activity. If children are playing housekeeping, talk about families and how God planned for us to live together in families. Be sure to include all types of families: two-parent families, one-parent families, families that include several generations, stepfamilies, foster families, extended families. Thank God for families.

- When preparing a meal or pretending to do so, talk about how God provides the food, and how God's helpers care for and take the food from the farms to stores for us to buy. Talk about how they are "preparing" the meal just as the students' parents take care of them by giving them food to eat. Thank God for those who help by giving us food.

- When building or working on a puzzle, or when reading a book, be alert to each child's developmental process. When a child is able to build a higher tower of blocks read new words, or piece together a puzzle that was frustrating on a previous day, talk about how he or she is growing, just the way God planned. Thank God for this new growth. This can be done with a simple statement: "I thank God for the way you are learning to stack the blocks."

Chapter 7

Creating Personal Prayers

Prayer is always personal, even when shared with other people. This chapter deals primarily with internal prayer, with personal conversations with God that need not be shared with others. There are many opportunities to nurture these prayers.

All children have worship experiences, even before they are old enough to verbalize what's going on inside. In fact, the lack of ability to verbalize may be one reason we often believe children are not able to worship at a young age. One day as I stood in a party store, a two-year-old boy hung onto his mother, whining, as she tried to talk to the clerk. In an effort to keep the child quiet, the clerk tied a helium balloon on the young boy's wrist. The clerk was unaware, however, that she helped to create a worship experience for that child. As I watched the boy slowly pull the balloon down and watch it rise again into the air, I saw an expression of awe or worship for the power that controlled the balloon, a power greater than his own.

We can lay the foundation for personal prayer with very young children even before they can understand the words. As you hold and rock or play with an infant, speak prayers of thanks and love for the child. This begins to set the tone for the child's reaction to prayer.

For preschoolers, personal prayers are sometimes verbalized even when no one else is around. Watch a three-year-old alone at play. Talking to him/herself, the child seems to carry on a conversation. Verbalization often helps the young child's thought process. Because of this, verbal direction or encouraging and enabling prayer may be particularly helpful for young children.

Jesus' Prayer Life

As you introduce personal prayer to older children and youth, talk about how Jesus taught us to pray by his example. Look at scriptures pertaining to Jesus' prayer life. In the classroom, divide the students into pairs. Have each pair read *one* passage. Suggest that the students also concentrate on a different passage each week at home.

Matthew 6:9b-13	**Luke 9:28-29**
Matthew 14:18-21	**Luke 10:21b-22**
Matthew 14:22-23	**Luke 23:34**
Matthew 19:13-14	**Luke 23:46**
Matthew 26:26-29	**Luke 24:30**
Matthew 26:36-43	**Luke 24:50-51**
Mark 1:35	**John 11:41b-42**
Mark 14:36	**John 12:27-28**
Mark 15:34	**John 17**
Luke 5:15-16	**John 21:13**
Luke 6:12-16	

As you look up the passages and recall the stories of Jesus' life, answer the questions below. In some instances you may need to read a few of the verses before and after the reference in order to answer the questions.

- When did Jesus pray? What was happening?
- Where was Jesus when he prayed?
- Who was with Jesus when he prayed?
- What kind of prayer did Jesus pray?
- Why do you think Jesus felt the need to pray?

Think about the last question and how this relates to our need to pray. Discuss what we learn about prayer from these examples of Jesus.

Silent or Meditative Prayer

Silent or meditative prayer may be a new idea to some people. Usually when we suggest silent prayer, we simply close our eyes and pray to ourselves. Sometimes we may give a suggestion of a subject for prayers, but we seldom direct the prayer. Just as memorized prayer is like practicing swimming strokes along the edge of a pool, a quiet inner communication with God can be compared to letting go and feeling the cool water support and refresh you on a hot summer day.

Marlene Halpin has done extensive work with children and prayer. In *Puddles of Knowing* (William C. Brown Company, 1984), she suggests that kindergarten and elementary children may compare praying to a milk stool. A milk stool has three legs, and all three legs must be the same length to keep balance.

We have three types of prayer, and they are all important for us to keep our balance. The first leg is private prayer or praying to God within yourself. This kind can be done anytime and anywhere. You only need God and yourself. The second leg is prayer in a small group such as your family or your class. The group is usually very special to you. The third leg is praying in corporate worship or a large group. This can happen with people you may or may not know. These prayers may be familiar because they are used often. Sometimes we call these liturgical prayers. At other times we pray in a large group, with one person leading the prayer and using his or her own words. But in corporate prayers we recognize our part in the bigger family of God.

The following exercise I have adapted from two sources: Halpin's book *Puddles of Knowing*, and *God Is with Us*, a media kit developed by Cecile Beam and published by Graded Press. The exercise will guide your students in personal or quiet prayer. You may substitute colors, trees, birds, flowers, or other things for the water. No particular body position is necessary, but everyone will need to be comfortable. Read the suggestions slowly and quietly, pausing to allow the students time to imagine.

First, I want you to find your own place in the room. You may want to sit or to lie down. It may be near someone else or in a corner by yourself, but you must have room to stretch your hands out without touching another person.

Imagine that you are in a private place, away from everyone else. What is your private space like? I think I'll paint mine blue. Do you want to paint yours? (*pretend to paint*) You can build a wall on all sides to make your place more private if you want. (*pretend to build*) Make a window in the wall if you like. Do you have cushions in your place? (*fluff up pillows*) Is it dark or bright?

Now I want you to close your eyes and imagine that you are a drop of water. Sometimes there may be other drops of water around you, and sometimes you may be alone. There is a rainbow overhead. Look at the different colors in the rainbow. Is it a complete rainbow, or do the colors dissolve into the air on one end?

Where are you as a drop of water? Imagine the place where you are. Are you in a river, moving slowly toward the ocean? Are you in a creek, laughing as you skip over rocks? Are you in a lake, or an ocean?

What is going on around you? Are there fish? Is an animal coming to drink? Are children playing? Are you turning a water wheel?

Now you change from running water to another type of water. How do you change? You decide how you will change and see it inside yourself.

What's happening to the other drops around you? What about the rainbow? What does it do?

(after a long pause) Now, let the imagining fade away. Come back to our classroom and be yourself, but remember how you felt.

(allow time for students to adjust back to the classroom) Would anyone like to tell us how you felt? You don't have to if you don't want to, because that was in your private place; but I would enjoy hearing about how some of you felt.

As volunteers tell of their feelings, ask them about what was happening in their imaginations as they had those feelings. Listen to each one and recognize each feeling as an OK feeling. Ask them occasionally where the rainbow was when they were having that feeling. If they don't know, you might suggest that they close their eyes again and go back into their imagining and let that part come. Take time for this.

The following meditation may be used after the quiet exercise above or independently. Tell the children that you are going to take some time for each of them to get to know the "really-really me" inside themselves. Ask them to close their eyes and relax. Next, ask them to listen to their own breathing as you say, "Breathe in; breathe out." Do this slowly at first, then faster, then slowly again. Then suggest the following:

First, I want you to think about yourself. Where is the "really-really me" part of yourself? Is the "really-really me" part your arm? Is it your foot? Is it your head? What part of you makes you laugh when you are happy, or cry when you are sad? What part of you loves, and what part feels great when you do something for someone else? That part is the "really-really me."

Now, take the "really-really me" part of you deep inside yourself. Take it into your heart. Invite God to come into your heart. Invite God to come into your heart with the "really-really me." Show God the special things about yourself. Show God anything else that you want to about yourself or about what has happened this week. (*pause long enough for private reflection*)

(*If this follows the exercise about the drop of water, add these sentences: "Show God how you felt as you imagined you were a drop of water. Show God what the rainbow did in your imagination."*)

Bring people who are special into your heart, too. Show them to God. Show God anything special about them. Are you having a special time? Is one of them having trouble? Is there something that you've talked to this special person about or something that you want to talk with him or her about? Tell God about how you love these special persons and about how they love you. Now let the "really-really me" and God love them together.

Let the thoughts of those people fade out of your mind, but continue to love them. Right now just God and the "really-really me" are in your heart. Let God love you. Think about how that love feels all around you. Enjoy just being with God.

Enjoy the love. Listen to what God may have to say to you. (*after a pause*) Open your eyes slowly. (*another pause*) Let's say together the prayer that Jesus taught us, "Our Father. . . ."

Sometimes you will want to use only the last part of this experience beginning with "Right now just God and the 'really-really me' are in your heart." Close that paragraph by asking everyone to listen to what God may have to say to him or her about some specific thoughts taken from experiences of the day or concerns in their family or community.

Your class may respond well to using this as a routine closing for your class period. Parents might want to use this exercise at a specific time each day.

With young children, use selected parts of the experience. Remember that their attention span is much shorter, and tailor the time accordingly. Older children and youth may use this prayer to identify the parts of prayer on page 13. For example, the thoughts about the rainbow may have spurred a prayer of adoration. Some of the students may have used the time to show God something about themselves or about their week as a prayer of thanksgiving or confession. When they brought people who were special into their hearts, they were praying prayers of intercession. Their time of listening to God may be a form of supplication.

Create a Special Place

Provide a quiet place in the classroom where individuals may go anytime they want for meditation. There are many ways that you can set up this place, but it is important that it be uncluttered. Change it frequently instead of putting all of your ideas into it at one time.

The quiet place may be created by moving furniture, draping material, or just piling fluffy pillows in a corner. Help children and youth feel free to use the quiet place from time to time. Add a few pictures or books that show God's world, or a record player and earphones for listening to instrumental music.

You may use a large basket of shells to encourage thoughts about how the animal that lived in the shell must have felt on the ocean floor. Or you might suggest looking at all the colors in the shell and feeling it to find its smooth and rough parts. Just holding the shell and wondering about it can lead to meditation and prayer.

Breath Prayer

Older elementary children and youth can work with creating a breath prayer, as suggested in the book *When I'm Alone,* by Ron DelBene (Upper Room, 1988). Quite simply, this is a prayer that may be said in one breath, breathing in and out. You may talk the process through with younger children.

What follows is an adaptation that I wrote for *Living Simply* (Abingdon Press, 1996), using the steps outlined in DelBene's book. Help initiate this prayer by asking your children or youth to close their eyes and think through the following steps.

1. Make yourself comfortable and quiet. Close your eyes. Remind yourself that God loves you and you are in God's presence. Recall a favorite poem or passage of scripture, such as "Be still, and know that I am God!" (Psalm 46:10).

2. Imagine that God is calling you by name. Listen carefully and hear God asking, "*(your name),* what do you want?"

3. Answer God with whatever comes honestly from your heart. Use one or two words or a short phrase in the answer, such as "Peace" or "I want to feel your forgiveness." If several ideas come out, combine or focus so that you find a specific need that is as basic to your spiritual well-being as water is to life. Ask yourself: *What do I want that will make me feel most whole?* Peace of mind and peace of heart will follow wholeness.

4. Choose a favorite name for God: *God, Jesus, Christ, Lord, Spirit, Creator.*

5. Combine your name for God with your answer to God's question *"What do you want?"* This becomes your breath prayer. It may be *"Let me know your peace, O God,"* or *"Jesus, I need to let go of troubles."* Try placing God's name at the beginning and at the end. One way may feel more comfortable than the other. Change the words as needed so that the sentence flows smoothly, as in a breath. Now say or think the words of the prayer as you breathe in and breathe out. Write the prayer down and use it several times during the day—in fact, any time you think it. Soon it will become a part of your life.[1]

Poetry Prayers

Very few of us have the talents of true poets, but we can all express ourselves in some sort of free verse. Experiment with various styles, and select several to try at different times. Typically, a person will enjoy one type more than another. After you have worked with several, encourage children and youth to choose their own style.

You may want to suggest the subject for the prayer poems, perhaps something that relates to what the child or youth has studied. It may be thanking God for something they have seen in God's world, or for people who are special to them. It may be thanking God for Jesus or for some truth learned from the Bible. It may be asking God to be near in a particular situation.

Examples of poems follow. Since this type of prayer requires reading and writing skills, the activities are most appropriate for older children and youth. However, they can be adapted for younger children by making it a group effort, with an adult writing the ideas down for the children.

1. **Picture poems** are words or phrases written in the outline shape of an object. If the prayer is for God's world, the student may elect to write the poem in the shape of a tree or a flower. If it is about how we change, you may suggest that the poem prayer be written in the shape of a butterfly. A Lenten prayer may be written in the form of a cross. Allow children and youth to decide on their own shapes as they become familiar with this method.

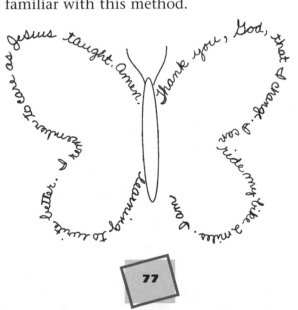

2. **The cinquain** *(sin cane)* poetic form has five lines. It is very effective for a prayer of thanks, or it may be a praise prayer. It may also be used as a request for help with a special problem.

Line 1: One word title or subject.
Line 2: Two words that tell about the subject. They may be a phrase or separate words.
Line 3: Three action words (verbs or "ing" words) or a phrase about the subject.
Line 4: Four words or phrase that tell of a feeling about the subject.
Line 5: The subject word again or another word that means the same. Or you may wish to use *Amen* here.

Here are two examples:

Trees
Leaves, branches
Swaying, rustling, reaching
A gift from God.
Shade

Name-calling
Unfriendly, unloving
Hurting, painful, distressing
I forgive and love.
Amen.

3. **Free verse** can take various forms. The lines may be any length. They may be phrases, sentences, or a series of words. With young children, suggest that they give you two short lines about something they are thankful for. Title it with the subject and add an *Amen* or *Thanks* at the end.

4. Children and youth enjoy **repetition**. Try creating a poem prayer by beginning each line with the same word.

Friends laugh with me when I'm happy.
Friends cry with me when I'm sad.
Friends love me even when I'm angry.
Friends are friends, no matter what.
Thank you, God, for friends.

The use of rap in a prayer also falls into this category. See page 92 for information on a rap prayer.

Another form of a repetition prayer repeats a short sentence every other line. The sentence may be about the subject, or it may be a response of praise or thanks.

I saw the pink sunrise this morning.
Thank you, God, for the colors.
A red bird flew by my window.
Thank you, God, for the colors.
I found yellow dandelions on the lawn.
Thank you, God, for the colors.
The bright blue sky became dark at night.
Thank you, God, for the colors.
Amen.

5. An **acrostic** prayer poem uses the first letters (and sometimes the last) of a line to form a word vertically down the page. Here is an example:

Thank you, God.
Help me to love others.
Always be with me.
Never let me forget you.
Know that I love you.
                    Amen.

6. Try a **pop-up** prayer poem. It has a few short sentences or phrases and just seems to pop into your mind. It can come after you have spent some time thinking about a subject or

just relaxing with God inside yourself. One of my pop-up prayers is this:

> O God,
> Fall is a time the world seems to die.
> But we come alive with
> > new schedules
> > new shirt sizes
> > new plans.
> Perhaps it's because we know
> > you are a dependable God.
> We know you send
> > new life each spring.
> > Amen.

7. Children and youth can relate to a prayer poem of the **senses.** This poem thanks God for a subject and tells about it using the five senses.

> Thank you, God, for my friend.
> I see her, and I am happy.
> I hear her voice; it sounds glad.
> I taste the lunch we share.
> I smell the flowers as we walk together.
> I feel important when I am with her.
> Thank you, God.

You can also make a prayer poem by using only one of the senses. It might be a prayer thanking God for food and describing how each food tastes. Or it might thank God for one of the senses.

> I hear the birds sing early in the morning.
> I hear the voices of my friends at school.
> I hear the noise of traffic.
> I hear the water as it fills the bath tub.
> I hear my mother (father) tell me "I love you."
> Thank you, God, for ears to hear.

Journaling and Prayer Notebooks

You may make journals or prayer notebooks with any age student. With young children, make a small booklet with pictures that tell about the prayer. Very young children may find pictures of favorite foods or of animals in magazines. If the child is too young to cut and paste, do this for them as they watch. Let them decide where they want to place the pictures in the book and arrange them on the page. They can help you push the picture into place and press it to make the paste stick. After you have pasted the pictures in the book, pray the prayer together, saying "Thank you God for. . . ." Have the child point to each picture so that he or she decides what you will thank God for. Older children may draw their own pictures.

Encourage children who can write to have a prayer notebook or journal they add to from time to time. You may even want this to be a part of a quiet time at the end of each class session or at home. Youth may want to journal what has happened to them during the past day or week. Stress the fact that the prayers may be in any form. They can even be a letter to God.

Assure the children or youth that the notebook is their own private prayer journal and that you will not read it. If they have something they want you to read at any time, they can bring it to you, but what they write in it is between them and God. The child or youth may want to draw a design on the cover or decorate it in some way. Consider making a prayer crest for the cover. You will find information on a prayer crest on page 85.

Youth may elect to put their prayers in a three-ring binder so they can add their own prayers as well as other prayers they discover that are helpful to them. Some of these may be prayers to memorize that can be quickly and easily prayed to give comfort and to express joy.

Make a special box or select a special drawer in your classroom where the notebooks will be stored.

Prayer Puzzles

Another creative way to help children form their own prayers is by giving them starters in puzzle form and then letting them add their own words. Puzzles give the framework for a prayer that students can build on. Here are a few to try, or you may create your own.

1. **Word Puzzle**   Similar to an acrostic prayer, use the letters in a word as the beginning letters of single words:

Everyone
Apples
Rivers
Trees
Home

For these I give you thanks, O God.

2. **Bouncing Ball Prayer Puzzle**   Fill in words in this prayer to make your own prayer:

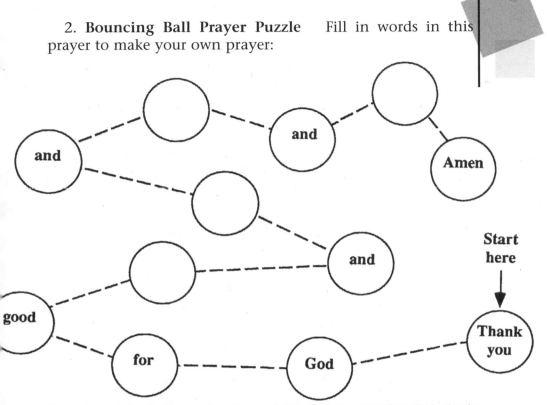

3. **Pyramid Prayer Puzzle**   Look at the sample on page 84. This prayer begins with one idea written on a large building block. One to three more blocks were added with nouns of that category written on each block. As the student thinks of words that are related to each of these nouns, additional blocks and words are added. You begin this prayer by reading from the bottom up.

The first time this type of puzzle is introduced to the class, do it together on the chalkboard and use just one or two categories until the students get the idea of how to do it. Consider providing a printed form with blank blocks and just the word idea and categories you wish to use. When the class is proficient, they can create their own pyramids. You can make this prayer more experiential by using wooden blocks and writing or taping the words on them.

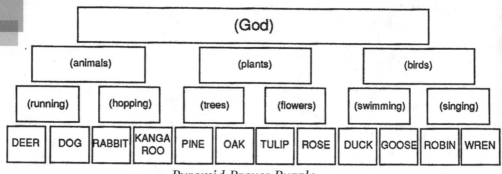

Pyramid Prayer Puzzle

4. **Overturned Prayer**   This prayer helps children and youth put themselves in the "shoes" of another. On three-by-five-inch cards, the children and youth will list something they enjoy, one on each card. Suggestions might include: *food that Mother cooks, playing with my friends, going to Sunday school, taking swimming lessons*, and so forth.

Next, ask them to write the first part of the prayer of thanks, using these ideas, and turn the card over to write what life would be like for someone who did not have them.

For example:

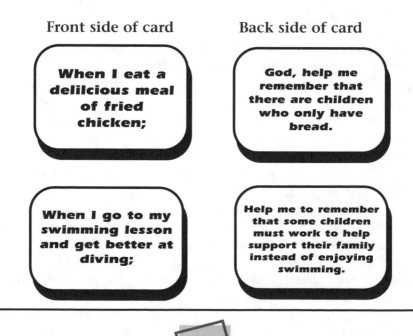

Front side of card

> When I eat a delilcious meal of fried chicken;

> When I go to my swimming lesson and get better at diving;

Back side of card

> God, help me remember that there are children who only have bread.

> Help me to remember that some children must work to help support their family instead of enjoying swimming.

5. **Prayer Path Puzzle**   Draw a path or road across a piece of paper. Add stepping stones. Provide the first few words of the prayer, putting one word per stepping stone. Duplicate the page for each child or youth to finish the prayer and decorate the page. When they become familiar with this form they can create their own Prayer Path Puzzle.

You may create a more permanent form by painting the prayer path on the floor or a sidewalk. You might even consider creating a prayer path through the yard, with stepping stones or signs along the way as reminders of things for which to pray.

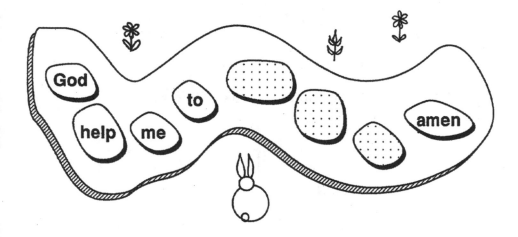

6. Personal Prayer Crest The crest has been used for many years to tell about a family or a community. It was particularly popular in Europe.

Give the students the following directions:

Using the crest shape, make a reminder of particular things you want to thank God for or that you want to talk with God about in your personal prayers. Write one subject in each space. Each time you pray, use the crest and talk with God about one or more of the subjects on your crest. Make new crests from time to time.

Consider creating a more elaborate crest from wood, with hooks in each section on which you can hang cards with prayer subjects.

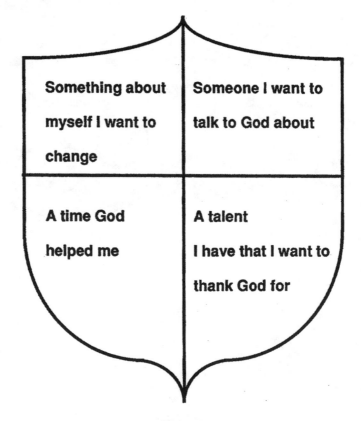

Something about myself I want to change

Someone I want to talk to God about

A time God helped me

A talent I have that I want to thank God for

Chapter 8

Creating Group Prayers

It is important for children and youth to experience a common bond between themselves and others, both in church and out. One of the foundations of a strong faith development is a relational experience with other Christians.

I have advocated to scores of church school teachers that if they do nothing else during the year but create a caring community among their students, they have accomplished much. God made us a relational people. God made us with a need to respond to each other and to our Creator.

Group or family prayers are one of the best ways to establish this relational experience. Group or family praying may be done using prewritten prayers such as those suggested in the chapter on memorized prayer. However, when prayers come out of the experiences of the group or family, a closer bonding of Christian love develops.

Conversational Prayer

Conversational prayer stems from conversation among the group or family members and listening to God's personal response. As adults, we participate in this sort of prayer often with a prayer circle. We ask if there are any special concerns that members want to lift up in prayer before the prayer time begins. Then we move around the circle, each person praying a few sentences, often about specifics that were suggested by the group members. Usually the leader sums up the prayer at the close of the meeting, praying for any concerns not mentioned by others.

This style of prayer can be threatening for those with little prayer experience because they feel pressed to pray. It is also a more formal prayer that some view as an endurance test. I suggest a more informal style of conversational prayer.

One of the best ways to initiate conversational prayer is to spend time talking together about the type of day or week that each person has experienced. Do not call this prayer, just conversation. Guide the conversation by using a beanbag featuring a different design on each side. One side will represent good things that happened, while the other not-so-good things. (Instead of *bad,* use the term *not-so-good* since it encompasses a broader range of experiences. What may seem "bad" to one person may not appear to be "bad" to another.)

As children move into an age where they can grasp the concept of cause and effect, they may see some of the good that comes from the not-so-good. This is the realization that we get from Romans 8:28: "We know that in all things God works for good with those who love [God], those whom [God] has called according to [divine] purpose."

It is best to sit in a circle for this prayer. This gives a better opportunity for open conversation. Allow the group to decide which side of the beanbag will be used to talk about the good things, and which for the not-so-good things. Explain that in your conversation everyone who would like to share will have the opportunity, but that in order for everyone to hear, only the person with the beanbag will talk.

Begin the conversation by placing the beanbag on the floor in front of you, with the appropriate side up, and sharing an experience you had. Toss the beanbag to someone else who would like to share. Each person who decides to do so will in turn place the bag on the floor with the appropriate side up as he or she tells about an experience.

Adults can appreciate such a conversation as a part of prayer, because we realize that God is with us always and knows all about our experiences anyway. However, students sometimes become inhibited at first when presented with the idea that this is part of our prayer. Simply begin sharing, and when everyone feels comfortable, say casually, "When we talk like this together, I'm sure that God is hearing us even before we say that we will pray. Perhaps this is a way of praying, too."

After everyone has had the opportunity to tell of their experiences, ask for the beanbag and place it in the center of the circle. Then close the time together with a simple prayer: "God, we come to you with many things that have happened recently, some of them good and some of them not-so-good. We thank you for being with us in all of these times. Amen."

As you work with conversational prayer you may find it appropriate to pause occasionally between sharing, particularly if something is shared that is particularly stressful. Let there be quiet time for silent prayers that lift the occasion up to God. Allow the students to listen to God within themselves instead of filling the space with words.

A Prayer Web

Creating a prayer web with yarn or string can help us recognize the way we relate to one another. This prayer provides an opportunity for everyone to contribute to a group prayer. Close with an inclusive sentence asking God to hear all that has been said. A prayer web is most appropriate for prayers of thanks. Or use another theme that is important to your group at that time.

Stand or sit in a circle. You may choose to sit on the floor. As you begin, hold on to the end of the string (or wrap it around your finger) and mention something you would like to thank God for or to pray about. Then ask if there is someone else who has something to add. Roll or throw the string ball to that person, making a string connection between you and that person. After sharing, that person will hold on to the string and roll/throw the ball to another. As you proceed across the circle, you will create a web with the string. If you are rolling the ball, ask everyone to hold the string high during the rolling; if throwing the ball, hold the string next to the floor.

After all who want to speak have shared, ask those who did not share to take hold of the string so that everyone is connected to the web. Close the experience with a simple sentence: "God, we ask you to hear all that we have talked about along our prayer web. Amen."

Preprayer Discussion

In order to create written group prayers, it is important to precede it with discussion. This discussion may start from a suggestion or a topic of interest to your students. You may even provide information for the students to research and then report on. Check your local library or various websites for information on your subject.

One such topic might be *hunger*. The following websites can provide information, and more can be found through a search engine on the Internet.

www.thehungersite.com
www.echonet.org
www.bread.org
www.gbgm-umc.org

If you are considering a topic such as *baptism*, provide materials on different uses of water for research before your discussion. If communion is your topic, research wheat and how bread nourishes us.

Summarize your discussion using the popcorn method. You will need a chalkboard or large sheet of paper for this. Ask persons to pop ideas about the subject to you in the form of words or short phrases. Randomly write these on the board or paper. Then, using these words or ideas, write a group prayer.

For example, one group did research in the book of Acts to find the characteristics of the early church. They decided that the church was (1) *devoted to learning*,

(2) *worshiped together*, (3) *enjoyed fellowship*, and (4) *shared among themselves and with others*. They then wrote a prayer asking God to help them develop those characteristics.

Litany Prayer

A litany is a form of prayer most often used in a group. In the litany, one or two lines are followed by a responsive phrase repeated by the entire group. This phrase is usually repetitive, although youth and children who read easily may enjoy some variation in the wording.

Children particularly enjoy litany prayers because they provide opportunity for verbal participation without the embarrassment of not knowing what to pray. When the litany is written by the children, they know the words before they offer the prayer. This takes away any pressure of thinking about what to say.

The litany grows out of personal feelings and concerns when it is written as part of a group experience. Printed litanies or ones prepared by one person are not as apt to reflect the personal feelings of the group.

Use the central theme for the litany as the title. Plan a theme and title that relates to your subject. As ideas on the theme of the litany are offered, write them on a large piece of paper or on the chalkboard. Then agree on a response. Consider scripture passages or a phrase from a song as the response. Write this on a separate paper. Organize the ideas into a pattern. Cut the statements apart and arrange them in order.

You may want to write a sentence of introduction for the worship leader, although it is not necessary. Use the litany for a worship experience. Tape strips with the statements together for reading, with the understanding that you will read the response between each statement. Place the names or initials of each person beside his or her contribution. When the litany is used in worship, ask each person to read his or her own contribution.

The litany is not a performance, not even when used before other people. Use simple language, even conversational tone. We want children and youth to look at prayer as a conversation with God.

The following example uses the theme of "Ways God Talks to Us." The leader, individuals, or small groups may read the sentences in regular print, and the total group reads the responses printed in boldface type.

Ways God Talks to Us Today

Leader: Jesus spoke to Paul on the road to Damascus, and God also speaks to us today. God speaks through the Bible.
We listen, God, as you talk.
Leader: Teachers and preachers tell us of God.
We listen, God, as you talk.
Leader: God talks to us through parents and friends.
We listen, God, as you talk.
Leader: We can hear God speak in the wind and in the quiet of the early morning.
We listen, God, as you talk.
Leader: God is within me and talks to my inner self.
Help me, God, to listen for you every day and at all times. Amen.[1]

Rap Prayers

Raps are very popular with children and youth. Raps appeal to those who lean toward rhythm in their learning, and few other methods within the classroom meet this need.

To create a rap prayer, have a preprayer discussion as suggested on page 90. Then follow these steps:

1. Write several short sentences about the subject.

2. Read each sentence and clap out the rhythm for each one. Remember that the rap or rhythm is spoken without music.

3. Do several of the sentences have similar rhythms? Select that rhythm and try to change the words of the other sentences to match that rhythm.

4. Come up with a summary phrase that can be repeated from time to time throughout the rap, such as "for <u>this,</u> we <u>pray,</u> O <u>God.</u>"

5. Practice the rap, adjusting the words or rhythm as needed. Underline the words that will beat the rhythm. Although you want to make the rap usable, remember that the praying actually happens as you create the rap. You are not looking for perfection!

6. Make plans to share the rap prayer with others.

Echo Pantomime

Echo pantomime is a popular method for teaching children, and can also be used effectively with youth and adults.

To create your own echo pantomime, divide a prayer into short phrases or sentences. (Young children will need to have their prayer broken frequently.) Consider a simple movement for each phrase or sentence. Practice the echo pantomime so that you have it in mind and feel comfortable with it before introducing it to others. You may find it helpful to write the pantomime on a large sheet of paper and post it high on the wall so that you can see it while facing everyone else. Older children and youth can create their own echo pantomime prayer.

Before using an echo pantomime for the first time, talk about what an echo is. Tell the students that in a pantomime we act something out. Explain that you will say a few words of the prayer with some actions, and they will repeat the words, using the same actions. Here is an example of an echo pantomime appropriate for younger children:

PRAYER	ACTION
Dear God, we thank you:	
For the sunshine.	Make large sun with both arms.
For the rain.	Moving fingers, lower hands.
For the trees that sway in the wind.	Sway like a tree.
For the grass and the flowers.	Put fingers together and move hands up, as if sprouts are coming through ground.
Sometimes we're happy;	Smile big and "draw" smile at corners of mouth with fingers.
Sometimes we're sad;	Frown and "draw" frown at corners of mouth with fingers.
But we know that you love us.	Fold arms across chest in "hug."
Amen.	Hands up, looking up.

Movement Prayers

When we include movement in our prayers, we are loving God with our whole selves, with our body as well as our heart and mind. Movement may be a part of the prayers that you create, or it may be adapted to printed prayers. Young children can participate in very concrete movements. Older children and youth can understand movement that symbolizes a feeling or an attitude. Some of our prayers from the early church heritage are more meaningful to children when we add movement to them. Prayer hymns are particularly easy to adapt to movement prayers.

Young children can enjoy making movements similar to an animal as they thank God for the animal. Or they may "sprout" from the ground as a blade of grass, or open their arms to the sunshine as a flower. They can curl up in a ball as if inside a seed, then let their hands form the sprout when the sun warms the ground. Encourage them to create their own movements. These can be simple thank-you prayers to God.

Older children and youth can experiment with movements ahead of time, then plan for a series of movements to use with the prayers. It is important that the students create and plan the movement as expressions of their feelings as the words of the prayer are said or sung. You can suggest movements and help them experiment until they find the movement they want.

Talk about the prayer and the meanings of the words. Ask them how they might express the meaning of a particular word or phrase without using words. Give them an opportunity to experiment and decide what movements they want to use.

When deciding which movements to use for particular parts of the prayer, remember that every word or phrase does not have to have a movement. Too many movements result in a prayer that is cluttered with action, and make it difficult to appreciate the meditative mood.

Be sure the movements are simple. Rather than a performance, the prayer is a communication between the participant and God. Never "practice" the prayer, but pray it. If one person expresses him/herself differently from another, welcome this as that person's own communica-

Approaching God	Step forward, head held high, arms down.
Praise	Uplifted head and upward movement of arms.
Receiving gifts; Holy Spirit	Head bowed, arms curved over head with fingertips touching
Communicating	Hand movement from lips upward as if to God, or outward as if to others.
Heaven and earth	One arm stretched up and in front; other arm stretched down and behind.
Whole universe	With right hand, circle left to right.
Springtime; new birth	Hands together at chest and then moving upward, as sprouts coming from earth.
Fellowship	Arms across neighbor's shoulder.
Unity	Clasping neighbor's hands.
Rejecting evil	Hands to sides, lowered and pushing back.
Repentance	Kneeling, looking above and then bowing head.
Amen	Head bowed, arms relaxed.

tion with God. Everyone does not have to do exactly the same thing.

On page 80 you will find some possible movements for your group.

Scripture Paraphrased Prayer

Paraphrasing is a good way to understand Scripture. Older children and youth are able to look up passages and work with paraphrasing by themselves. With younger children, read the verse together and talk about how you could say the same thing in different words. The paraphrased scripture can then be used in a prayer. You may want to create a litany prayer with it. Here are examples of prayer created from paraphrased verses:

God Brings Growth

God made everything and was happy with it. (Genesis 1:31)
Thank you, God, for your plan for growth.

God has a time for everything. (Ecclesiastes 3:1)
Thank you, God, that we grow from babies to adults.

To be a friend, we always love. (Proverbs 17:17*a*)
Help us, God, to remember our friends.

Be loving to each other. Forgive each other as Christ taught. (Ephesians 4:32)
We will try to use our actions to produce good feelings, dear God.

It is good to grow up in all ways. (Ephesians 4:15)
Our minds continue to grow no matter what our age. Thank you, God.

We are shown God in many ways. (Deuteronomy 4:35*b*)
We thank you, God, that we understand more about you each day.
Thank you, God, for growth.

                         Amen.

Table of Thanks

Set aside a table as a praise table or table of thanks. Make a large sign, and illustrate it with gifts from God.

On the table, place a few objects that remind us of gifts for which we can thank God. They may be food gifts, gifts from nature, gifts of relationships, or gifts of love from other people. Suggest that everyone look for and bring symbols of gifts to place on the table.

Plan to spend time at the table talking together about God's gifts that are displayed. Offer thanks in prayer, asking persons to mention something from the table between a phrase such as "Thank you, God, for your gift of _____."

Flat Pictures Prayer

Assemble a number of pictures on a particular subject. These may be from magazines or from your church school picture file. Spread the pictures out on the floor and ask each person to select one picture that reminds him or her of something he or she would like to talk to God about in your group prayer.

For younger children, you might make this a thanksgiving prayer. The pictures may show food, clothing, animals, parents, and so forth. Use statements and questions such as these to explain the process:

- Select a picture that shows something you like very much. You can pretend that the pictures of people are special people that you like.
- I would like for you to tell us something about your picture. (Allow each person to share as he or she is ready, but do not insist on anyone talking who doesn't want to.)
- These are special things and people that God has given us. Let's thank God for them: "Thank you, God, for all you have given us. Amen."

Elementary-age children and youth could consider our responsibility to take Christ to all the world, and develop an intercessory prayer for persons in other countries. Use pictures of persons from other countries. Adapt the following statements and questions to the pictures you have available:

- Select a picture from those laid out.
- In what ways does that person look like you?
- How is he or she different?
- Look at where the person is. How is it alike or different from where you live?
- Do you suppose the person in your picture speaks English? If not, how do you think he or she feels when he or she hears English?
- Does she or he look happy or sad? What do you suppose made him or her happy or sad?
- If you could talk with the person, what would you say?
- What favorite Bible story might you tell him or her?
- Let's pray a prayer of intercession, remembering the people of other countries, trusting them to God and asking God to show us how we can help them: "Our God, we cannot go to other countries now to personally share the stories of Jesus with these people. But we want them to feel very near to you. We know that they have some problems like ours and some that are different from ours. We know that you can help them, and we will help by sending others to share with them. Amen."

A mission project for your family or class may grow out of this prayer.

Older children and youth can use pictures to stimulate and focus meditation. Pictures of people in life situations are good for this. Here is an example of questions and statements you might use to guide them:

- From the selection of pictures, choose one.
- What do you think happened just before this picture was taken?

- Look at one person in the picture. Give the person a name.
- How do you think your person is feeling?
- What do you think your person's needs are?
- Say a prayer for your person.
- What are some things that could have happened in the next few minutes after the picture was taken?
- Introduce your person to the group. (Each person, as he or she is ready to do so, holds his or her picture so all can see it and starts by saying, "This is [Mary]. She [he] . . .")

After the meditation, close with a simple prayer asking God to help us all be more sensitive to the needs of those around us.

Chapter 9

Creating Prayers Using Art

No two people learn the same things from the same experience. The research on multiple intelligence on page 41 points this out. If we are to teach prayer, then we must be prepared to introduce prayer using a variety of methods.

Creating original prayers with art is natural with children. As we grow older, we often suppress our creativity and become inhibited. Conversations can foster creativity. Acceptance of a person's work can encourage creativity. Use art as a means of helping to encourage the search for God within, then use the art expression as a way to help children and youth share the thoughts they had as they were creating.

It is important to consider art as a method of praying, rather than an achievement of a finished product for display. The simple act of creation lays a foundation for a deeper relationship with our Creator-God. I so often have to remind myself, when working with children, "It is in the doing that the growing occurs, not in the finished product." Naturally, we want children to have pride in their art expression, but we need to realize that we are not teaching an art class. Use art as a tool and allow each person to work with the art at his or her own pace and own way.

When we consider art as a tool, we keep the prayer environment fresh and active. In the classroom, very little art needs to be displayed for more than a few weeks. Much of it could be better appreciated if taken home, where students could see their work every day of the week. It then acts as a reminder that God is with them each day, and that we can pray to God anywhere.

First, experiment with the method yourself. This is particularly important with art. Although each method suggested here will have a list of materials, by experimenting you will be sure that you are prepared. *(NOTE: Try to avoid the use of food as you work with art. When we use food as non-food items and later try to initiate concern for people who are hungry, we are sending mixed signals. We are saying on one hand that food is important and should not be wasted, and then saying on the other hand that it is OK to waste food by gluing it to a picture.)*

In the classroom, art is used in most curriculum as a way of responding to what was learned. Since we are accustomed to focusing on achievement, we will need to work on shifting the students' focus from their finished creation to their experience and feelings as they use the art medium. As I suggested earlier, there is no requirement that we bow our heads and close our eyes to pray. As we consider various artwork and create it we are actually praying.

You can make these prayer experiences different from the ordinary art project by encouraging persons to talk about the feelings they had as they worked. When making comments during the experience, begin with a positive statement about the piece, but move on to conversation about the feelings that the person is having or what he or she is thinking during the process.

As you display the art prayers, talk about how they remind us of "what we thank God for" or of "how we want to ask God to help us." This focuses on the experience instead of the finished project. When the students take their artwork home, suggest that they use it to remember the prayer they learned in class and pray it at home. Encourage them to pray the prayer with their family. If it is a personal prayer, suggest that they place it in their room where they can see it and pray the prayer before they get out of bed in the morning, or at night before they go to sleep.

Picture Prayers

Drawing or painting pictures is such a common art project that we often think of it *as* art. Because it requires so little preparation time, it is often overused or used with little preparation. Since each person learns differently, be sure that you use a variety of art methods with prayer and do not overuse drawing or painting in a group. When you recognize that a particular art form is effective with a particular child or youth, encourage its use.

Recognize that creating a picture is placing a part of yourself on the paper. This part of self is very important. It is a part of the person's individualism and self-esteem. When talking with a child about the picture, begin with a positive expression such as: "You have used such lovely colors in the picture. Will you tell me about it?" What they see clearly in their drawings we may mistakenly think is something else. Therefore it is important to invite the child to interpret the picture first. Then you will want to encourage conversation about feelings or thoughts that he or she had during the creating process.

Use research or conversation as preparation for drawing. If you work with a prayer of thanks, talk about God's creation or about friends and helpers for which we are thankful. Picture prayers can also be used as you pray about relationships between people. These may include pictures of friends playing together happily, or older children or youth may draw a picture of a problem in a relationship that he or she wishes to talk with God about. The drawing experience itself becomes the prayer. While drawing, the mind and the heart are active in the process. The praying takes place within.

Materials needed:
❑▶ Paper (size depending on use)
❑▶ Crayons, markers, chalk, or tempera paints and brushes

Finger Painting

Finger painting adds the dimension of movement to the experience of painting, and this can help to make the prayer internal. It can be especially effective for those who learn best kinesthetically (see page 41).

Finger painting is an ideal method to use during a guided meditation. If you only give guidance beforehand and do not guide the thoughts during the prayer, then you may want to play music as the students pray.

If you have never used finger paints before, allow time for experimentation before you begin to talk about the prayer. First use of finger paints always brings strange comments, and it is better that these comments be aired ahead of time so that everyone can then focus on the thoughts of the prayer.

Most children enjoy finger painting, but some parents have made such a strong issue over the importance of "keeping clean" that the child cannot experience the joy of finger painting for fear he or she will meet disapproval from the parent. In the classroom, use your own judgment in such cases.

Don't push any art experience onto a child. If he or she refuses, suggest that he or she sit and watch the others and think about the prayer silently, or provide another form of art expression for the child.

We often think finger painting is just for very young children, but finger paint, music, and a suggested topic can produce a very meaningful experience for older children, youth, and even adults.

Finger painting requires a thicker paint than other forms of painting. There are commercial finger paints on the market, or you can make your own by adding a little dry tempera to liquid starch.

Some preschools have used puddings as finger paints; however, avoid sending children mixed signals about the importance of food.

Materials needed:

- ❏▶ Finger paint
- ❏▶ Finger paint paper or shelf (shiny) paper, or a smooth surface such as cookie sheets or trays
- ❏▶ Old shirts or smocks to protect clothing

Prepare the paper or surface by dampening it with a sponge. If you are using paper, wetting the surface also helps the paper stay in place. Place the shiny side of the paper up. Place a few tablespoons of the paint on the paper or surface. To finger paint, move the paint around with your fingers to make pictures, designs, or impressions. You may also use the fist, palm, or even forearm. (Be sure sleeves are rolled or pushed up out of the way.)

Stained-glass Prayers

Stained-glass windows were first placed in churches at a time when most ordinary people could not read. They served as reminders, or symbols, of Bible stories and of biblical concepts. By looking at the windows, the people could recall the stories they had been told.

Creating an object that looks like a piece of stained glass is an exciting way of praying. Symbols lend themselves well to this medium.

Materials needed:

- ❏▶ White paper (typing weight)
- ❏▶ Black construction paper
- ❏▶ Pencils, crayons, and scissors
- ❏▶ Black permanent marker
- ❏▶ Glue
- ❏▶ Cooking oil
- ❏▶ Cotton swabs
- ❏▶ Table protection and paper towels

Precut frames from black construction paper, cutting out the space where the picture will show through.

After conversing about the subject of your prayer, discuss possible ways to illustrate the prayer. Place the precut black construction paper frame over the paper and draw an outline of the opening. (After the picture is finished, the "opening" area will be treated with oil, but the area outside the "opening" will be left white and not treated with oil.) Inside the open area, draw the symbol or picture outline with pencil, and trace over it with black permanent marker. This will represent the "leaded" part of the stained glass. Using crayons, color all parts inside the "opening" area, including the background.

Protect the working surface with papers. Using cotton swabs dipped in cooking oil, coat the backside of the colored area of the paper, being careful not to use the oil outside the colored area. Wipe any excess with paper towels.

Spread glue on the white, unoiled areas of the paper and then press the black construction frame to the glued areas. *(NOTE: To adapt this for young children, you may need to make several patterns of symbols that a child may select from, such as foods that we are thankful for. You will have to help the child trace the pattern and fill in the permanent markings.)*

Poster or Banner Prayers

Posters or banners are more permanent reminders of prayer. You may want to use this medium to share your prayers with the rest of the church or to hang them at home for a period of time.

Materials needed:
- ❑▶ Large pieces of heavy cloth such as felt or heavy rolled paper (Cut to make individual banners fifteen by eighteen inches or smaller.)
- ❑▶ For cloth banners: medium to small pieces of multicolored, multitextured cloth, lace, rick-rack, and so forth.
- ❑▶ For paper banners: crayons, markers, tempera paint, or colored paper
- ❑▶ Glue (white or fabric glue), needles, and thread
- ❑▶ Scissors and pencils
- ❑▶ Large paper for planning sketches; grocery sacks for patterns
- ❑▶ Hanging device such as dowel sticks or broom handles and string or cord (masking tape for paper banners)

Here are several ways to create and use banners:

1. The banner may be a prayer of adoration. You might talk first about parts of God's world that remind you of the greatness of God. Each person may make his or her own banner, selecting one of these things as the center of the design, or you may incorporate several ideas into one banner. Or you might make a banner using stylized designs of ways that we praise God. The line drawings in the Good News Translation are an excellent source for this. In the future, you may use the banner to focus your minds on a prayer of adoration.

2. Prayers of thanksgiving can come from a banner experience. These naturally follow conversations about

things for which we are thankful. They may be people, God's world, experiences, foods, and so forth.

3. Concern for others can be a center focus of a banner. This becomes an intercessory prayer. It may follow a study of persons in another country or people in need in your own city. The banner may be as simple as hands reaching out to each other, or it might display photographs taken around your neighborhood.

Select your theme and jot down words, shapes, and colors that remind you of this idea. Make drawings on paper of how the words and shapes might fit together, deciding on your basic design.

If you are making a cloth banner, make a full size paper pattern for each color. You will also want to make patterns for the letters of any words you plan to use. These are then moved about on the background fabric to get a better idea of how the finished product will look. For paper banners, pencil in the design and color it last.

Pin the patterns on the appropriate colored pieces of fabric and cut them out. Glue or sew them in place. You may wish to attach other decorations such as braid, buttons, and so forth.

The top of the banner may be finished with a hem large enough to hold the wooden dowel, and a string or cord tied to both ends of a dowel. The bottom may be finished by hemming, cutting scallops or points, or attaching a fringe. The banners may be used in prayer times at home or in a classroom to focus your prayers. If you have developed a quiet place, include a banner in it, but change it periodically so that fresh prayer thoughts come from the banners. You may also be able to use the banner in the sanctuary for special worship services.

Prayer Collage

A collage offers a three-dimensional expression of prayer, using an assortment of items that may be attached to a surface. It may be done as a group prayer, or each person may prepare individual prayers.

Materials needed:

❑▸ For background or surface: construction paper, cardboard or box tops, pieces of wood, paper plates, and so forth

❑▸ Assortment of items for selecting, such as various colored or textured paper to be cut or torn into shapes; straws; egg shells; cotton balls; fabrics; lace; fur or leather scraps; small stones; shells; wood shavings; dried grasses and seeds; packing materials; buttons; and so forth

❑▸ White glue or other strong glue

Begin by exploring the variety of materials you have provided for the collage. Spend some time talking about specific items and what they remind the students of, or feelings that they have when they see or touch the items.

If you are creating a thank-you prayer, you might consider thanking God for textures and create a collage of various textures. Talk about how some things are rough and some are smooth. Some things are smooth and rough, such as an ear of corn. God created all sorts of textures.

Another prayer might include persons who are a part of the child's or youth's life. The objects might symbolize these persons or ways that the persons care, such as a bit of rick-rack to remember that Mother made a dress, a piece of sponge to recall how a sister or brother helped clean up after an accident, a piece of wood shaving to remember the toy that Grandfather made, or shells to remember the enjoyable time that the family had at the beach. This prayer activity should be planned a week in advance so that items may be brought from home to use in the collage. Plan to have supplemental items or objects available for new ideas, as well as for visitors and others who may need materials.

Once the items have been selected for the collage, experiment with ways to arrange them on the background material. Any preparation of the background material, such as sanding or painting, will need to be done before the items are attached. Attach the items to the collage using white glue, or use a stronger glue for heavy articles.

Prayer Mosaic

Mosaics are pictures or designs from a collection of similar objects. A prayer mosaic may be made after conversing about some particular subject, or you may suggest that each person selects his or her own subject for prayer and make a mosaic that tells about the prayer.

Materials needed:
❏▶ Rigid background piece: cardboard, plywood, boards, linoleum, Styrofoam, or hard plastic
❏▶ Materials to be arranged for design: paper (small pieces of colored tissue, construction paper, wrapping paper, and so forth), shells, pebbles, small pieces of cloth, colored egg shells (broken or crushed), buttons, nut shells, seeds, bark, and so forth (See page 102 about the use of food items such as rice or beans.)
❏▶ White glue

With a pencil, sketch the design on the background material. The most accessible objects to use to fill in the design are small pieces of colored paper. Grouping the colors, glue the pieces on the background to form the picture or symbols.

For small children use larger pieces and glue them to outline the symbols or pictures rather than fill the piece in completely. Remember that the attention span for young children is short, and they will tire easily if they must fill in large areas of the mosaic.

Prayer Chain

Paper chains have been favorites with children for as long as we have had paper and glue. Generally, we have used them primarily for Christmas decorations, but there is no reason not to combine this favorite creative activity with prayer.

Materials needed:
❏▶ Construction paper of various colors, cut into strips about one by six inches
❏▶ Glue or tape

During a discussion on the prayer subject, or during a time of private reflection, each person will write or draw specific items for prayer, one item on each strip of paper. Then the strips are made into a chain by interlocking them and taping or gluing the ends of the strips together with the words and/or drawings on the outside. By using the chain, the person remembers what he or she decided to include in the prayer. Each day a different link is chosen to help focus prayer.

This method may also be used for a group prayer. Each person would have one strip of paper and write on it one item to be included in the group prayer. Then as you pray each person mentions his or her item, and the group responds with a sentence such as "We thank you, God" as the strip is attached to the chain.

Prayer Mobile

A mobile is a useful experience in prayer that can serve as a reminder during daily prayers. Young children will need assistance in assembling a mobile, but they can take part in the selection of the items to make up the mobile. The older the child, the more capable he or she is of completing the mobiles him/herself.

Materials needed:
- ▶ Hangers for the mobile: dowel sticks, cardboard paper rolls, wire, small tree branch, coat hangers, or paper plates
- ▶ String or yarn for hanging objects
- ▶ Objects to be hung from mobile
- ▶ Scissors, glue, and so forth, depending on your objects

A prayer mobile may have objects or pictures that are symbolic of the subjects for which you will pray, or it may be made up of the words that will be used in the prayer itself. If you are drawing pictures or using symbolic objects, talk about what the objects or pictures tell us about the subject. Young children may search for pictures to cut out that remind them of what they want to pray about, such as food, animals, friends, and so forth. If you are using words, encourage each person to think of his or her own words.

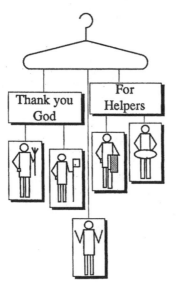

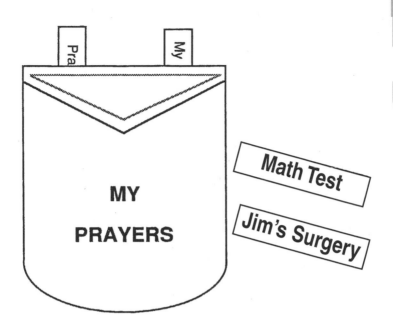

Prayer Pocket

A prayer pocket can contain ideas and thoughts that the person may want to include in his or her prayers. Write thoughts out on paper, to be placed in the pocket.

Materials needed:
- ☐▶ An envelope that has not been used (your choice of size, but consider one small enough to fit inside a Bible)
- ☐▶ Crayons or felt markers for decorating the envelope
- ☐▶ Strips of paper about one and a half by five inches

Turn the envelope so that a shorter side is at the top. If the envelope opens along the long side, seal it and cut it open on the short side that is at the top. Decorate the envelope so that it looks like a pocket, drawing symbols, flowers, and so forth, on it.

As you talk about what might be included in a prayer, ideas can be written on the strips of paper (or pictures cut from magazines) and placed in the Prayer Pocket. During a prayer time, each person will look through his or her Prayer Pocket and privately pray for what he or she has included. Encourage them to place the Prayer Pockets in their Bibles and use them daily. They can add other prayer thoughts to the Pocket, and if something is no longer appropriate, they can take that out.

Youth may make book covers (paper or fabric) for their Bibles and attach a prayer pocket to the front of the cover.

Prayer Mat of Woven Paper

A favorite paper craft among children is weaving strips of paper. This can be used in much the same way you would use paper chains in prayer, to help us remember what we want to pray about. Elementary age children and youth might recognize paper weaving as symbolic: as Christians, we believe that God uses all things (or weaves together all things) for good. If the strips represent persons for whom you will pray, then the woven prayer may symbolize how we all relate to each other as Christians.

Materials needed:
❑▶ Strips of paper of two colors
❑▶ Pencils for writing on paper strips

As you consider what is to be included in prayer, write items on the strips. These are then woven together. Place all strips of one color side by side on the table. Taking one strip of the other color, weave over and under those on the table. The first strip may be stapled, taped, or glued in place in order to stabilize the others. The other strips will be left free so that individual strips may be removed and read for prayer and then replaced.

Encourage the children and youth to place the prayer mat in their Bible so that they can use it when they read their Bible and have a personal time with God.

Prayer Cube

The prayer cube is another physical way to remember items you wish to include in your prayer. You may wish to use general ideas for this instead of specifics. There will be six sides to the prayer cube; each person will decide on six different categories he or she wants to include in prayer. They may include things such as food, God's world, family members, friends at school, relationships with peers, decisions to be made, ways to help others, our church and church school class, ways we grow/change, and so forth.

Materials needed:
- ❏▶ Square box, poster weight paper, or cardboard
- ❏▶ Crayons or felt markers
- ❏▶ Glue or tape if making cube from paper or cardboard

If you can locate a square (or almost square) box, use it. If not, cut out the cube using the drawing as a guide. The cube should be at least three inches square. If you are making a group cube, make it larger. Wait until the drawings are complete before assembling the cube.

Each surface on the cube will feature a drawing, words, or symbol representing a category for prayer. If you use boxes, create these drawings on paper and then cut it to fit each surface.

After the drawings are complete, glue each picture to a surface. If you construct cubes using the design above, make the drawings directly on the cube surfaces, then glue or tape the cube together according to the instructions on the illustration.

For example, one older elementary class made a prayer cube for their classroom. Each side represented something they usually included in their class prayer: an insight that Jesus provided, something they had learned from the

Bible, persons who were sick or lonely, a program of their church, a caring person, a gift from God. During their closing prayer time, a child took the prayer cube, prayed about one category, and then set it in the middle of the circle. Another child picked up the cube and prayed about another category and set it down. This continued until everyone who desired to had the opportunity to pray.

If someone is handy with carpentry, you might have a larger cube made from wood. Then paint symbols or attach pictures to the cube. Or consider purchasing large wooden square boxes for this purpose. Such cubes could be reused by painting a solid color over the original pictures and applying new pictures.

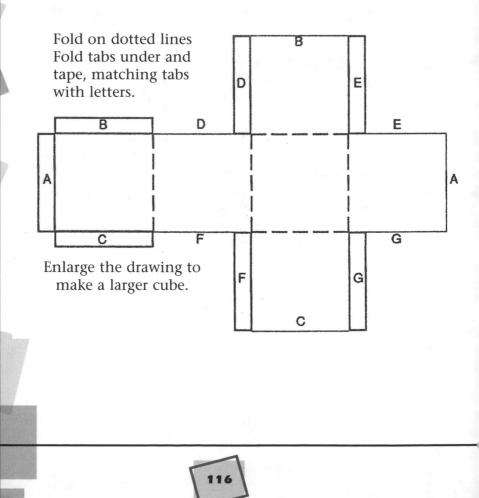

Fold on dotted lines
Fold tabs under and
tape, matching tabs
with letters.

Enlarge the drawing to
make a larger cube.

Slide or Filmstrip Prayers

This method can be used when you create a group prayer. You may either create a slide prayer by using photo slides that illustrate your prayer, or you may create your own slides or filmstrips using write-on matte acetate material produced for this purpose. If you make your own, be sure that each person makes at least one slide or one frame for the filmstrip.

As you plan your prayer, talk about just what you will want to include. Will it be a prayer that includes several different subjects, or will it be centered around one specific theme? What pictures, words, or symbols might be appropriate for the prayer?

Write the prayer, using some of the methods suggested in the chapter on creating group prayers. Then decide what parts of the prayer you will want to illustrate with the slides or filmstrip.

Materials needed for creating your own slides or filmstrip:
❑▶ Old filmstrips and bleach or 35mm write-on-film from an audio-visual equipment dealer or school supply store

OR

❑▶ Slide mounts (sold commercially) and tracing paper; or check your school supply store or an audio-visual equipment dealer for write-on slides
❑▶ Colored ballpoint pens, fine-tipped permanent markers, or transparency pens and pencils
❑▶ Projector

If you use an old filmstrip, place it in bleach to remove the color. After it has bleached, rinse thoroughly in clear water. Hang it up to dry, placing a clothespin or some other heavy object on the bottom of the filmstrip to be sure that it dries without curling.

Draw a line across the film at every fourth hole. This will mark off the frames. Draw the illustrations in these frames in order according to your prayer. Allow each drawing to dry before touching to keep from smearing the design.

If you are making your slides from scratch, mark off a section on tracing paper just slightly smaller than the size of the slide mounting. Inside this marking, draw the limits of the "window" part of the mounting. Draw and color illustrations for the prayer within the "window" marking on the tracing paper. Cut the picture the size of the outside marking and center the picture so that it shows through the "window" of the slide mounting. Glue or snap the mounting together. Arrange the slides in sequence for the prayer.

If you are using write-on slides or filmstrip material, draw directly on the matte acetate. Using projection pens and pencils will give you color when projected. These pens and pencils also enable you to "erase" by using a damp tissue.

Computer Prayers

Computers are becoming so commonplace that even two-year-olds can use them in some instances. Depending on your own skills and the skills of your children and youth, you can do everything from writing a prayer with word processing software, to making a prayer book or even creating a slide prayer using Microsoft® PowerPoint® software. Rather than trying to give detailed instructions on the use of the computer, I suggest reading one of the books on computers listed in the resource list and apply the ideas to forming prayers. You can also find websites with prayers that you can download.

Photo Prayer Book

A photo prayer book can be made by an individual or a class. If you create one as a class, on one Sunday plan the contents of the book. On the next Sunday take the photos, and, after developing the film, the book may be put together on the third Sunday. If you have a longer class period, the first two sessions may be combined; and if you use a digital or Polaroid-type camera you may complete it in one session.

Materials needed:

❑▶ Camera that is simple to operate and film (Or if a digital camera is used, the pictures can be saved, downloaded to a computer, and then printed.)

❑▶ Scrapbook and photo mounting materials

The photo prayer book will be used more as a reminder of specific things to include in personal prayer. However, you will want to have some conversation about what to include.

After planning what to include in the book, take photos to illustrate the prayers. The photos may be of elements found in nature, or of specific people such as church helpers, or community agencies such as hospitals and nursing homes that care for people, and so forth. Some students may even want to dramatize specific relational situations to be photographed, such as fighting and forgiving, shunning and friendship, ignoring and helping, and so forth.

When the photos are developed, write captions for each photo in the prayer book. Use the book spontaneously throughout the year. You may want to make several books throughout the year, using various themes.

Chapter 10

Musical Prayers

> Clap your hands for joy, all peoples!
> Praise God with loud songs!
> —Psalm 47:1

Singing has been a part of our religious heritage for thousands of years. It is a natural part of our response to God, and rightly so, for God created music and God created us. God gave us the ability to respond to and create music with movement, with instruments, and with our voices.

When our son was a preschooler, he loved to sing. His songs had great enthusiasm but very little tune. He would sing along with us, and I thought, *Poor child, he must be tone deaf because he doesn't stay on key.*

Shortly before Sam's sixth birthday, we visited my aunt and uncle. Aunt Elizabeth was much more musical than I, and she asked him to sit with her at the piano. She played a note and asked Sam to sing it. When he was not on key, she suggested that he listen to the sound and move his voice up or down until he hit the right note. Sometimes she helped him by playing the note he was singing on the piano, then moving up or down the scale.

Amazingly, Sam had never realized that there was any reason to move his voice around and find the right note. He had just sung random notes for joy! With Aunt Elizabeth's twenty-minute start, he went on to sing in All-State Chorus two years in high school and play trombone in All-State Band. He can now listen to a tune and write the notes, like someone else would take shorthand. Music has become a part of his life ministry.

When my father was a child, he was told that he shouldn't sing because he couldn't sing on key. As a pastor, he led many hymns from the pulpit without singing very loud until a music director in our church convinced him to sing with the choir in *Messiah*. For years he had missed this joyful expression of praise and prayer because someone had squelched his joy for singing during his childhood.

Singing Prayers

Some people do not know much about music and feel uncomfortable leading it. But it is important that we nurture in children and youth the joy of expressing themselves through song. Our challenge is not to teach music, but rather to help them praise God and pray in many ways. And singing is an appropriate experience of praise and prayer.

If you do not feel comfortable singing yourself, ask someone else to tape the songs for you, and use the tape as you sing prayers. Use various musical accompaniments where possible, and sometimes use no accompaniment. Some people sing better with one accompaniment or another. For quick reference, place only one song on a side of the tape and label it.

If you are teaching a class and feel uncomfortable about using music, find someone in the church who will help you from time to time as you incorporate music and prayer. Be sure that the person realizes that your goal is not a perfect voice blend, but an opportunity for expression through singing.

There are many prayer songs available in songbooks. Songs are also printed in children's take-home leaflets. Begin a collection of prayer songs for future reference.

The hymnal is another good source of prayer songs. It is important to help children who take part in congregational worship become familiar with those songs your congregation uses frequently. Some are prayers of joy and praise, and some are prayers asking God for help or forgiveness. Consider the hymns your congregation uses and read through the words of the hymn, remembering the age of the child or youth. Some words are too abstract for young children, even with explanation. With young children, you may want to use only a few phrases that are appropriate. Look over the following list of commonly used hymns to sing as prayers.

Come, Thou Almighty King
Holy, Holy, Holy! Lord God Almighty
Joyful, Joyful, We Adore Thee
For the Beauty of the Earth
Breathe on Me, Breath of God
Have Thine Own Way, Lord
O Master, Let Me Walk with Thee
Take My Life, and Let It Be Consecrated
Lord, Speak to Me
Dear Lord and Father of Mankind
Open My Eyes, That I May See
Lord, I Want to Be a Christian
Break Thou the Bread of Life (often used in communion)

Your hymnal will also have responses and blessings that you sing frequently in your church. Use them in your classroom so that children and youth can participate in worship with meaning. Some of these may include

Be Present at Our Table, Lord
Glory Be to the Father (Gloria Patri)
Praise God, from Whom All Blessings Flow
(Doxology)
God Be in My Head (Sarum Primer)
Lord, Have Mercy Upon Us (Kyrie Eleison)

The psalms are a good source of prayer songs. Check the scripture index of your hymnal for songs that are based on psalms. The source of the words of a hymn is printed on the page with the hymn. Some familiar ones are

> O Lord, Our Lord, in All the Earth (Psalm 8)
> The Heavens Declare Thy Glory, Lord (Psalm 19)
> Mountains Are All Aglow (Psalm 65:9-13)
> O God, Our Help in Ages Past (Psalm 90)
> Praises My Soul, the King of Heaven (Psalm 103)
> Rejoice, Ye Pure in Heart (Psalms 20:4 and 147:1)

You can help create music to sing with the psalms or with your own prayers. You may want to create a singing response to a prayer litany you have written. Here are some suggestions that will help you get started.

1. Taking one phrase of the prayer at a time, say or read the phrase together, feeling the "pulse" and developing a rhythm.
2. Ask various people in the group to speak the phrase individually, using the same rhythm. Talk about how different voices make the phrase sound differently even when you are using the same words and rhythm. Talk about the "color" sound of each voice, asking what color the voice sounds like. Recognize that God gave us all unique "colors" or sounds in our voices. Affirm the uniqueness of each person's voice.
3. As you go through the phrase again, ask everyone to listen to the rise and fall of the voice. Tell them that this can be duplicated with music.
4. Ask if someone can think of a tune that might go with the phrase. Allow time to think. You may want to suggest a central tone, using whatever instrument you may have on hand. Use the key of C for simplicity, and play the chord C, E, G.
5. Using the suggested tune, sing the phrase together several times.

6. Move on to the next phrases in the same procedure, but repeating the whole song periodically so that you can see how one phrase moves to another.

Another easy way to create a song prayer is to use a familiar tune, such as "Are You Sleeping, Brother John," and think of words that you may use with that music. Here are some words for this tune. After a bit of practice, write your own words.

> Lord, we thank you; Lord, we thank you
> For our food, for our food.
> You have loved us always; you have loved us always.
> > A-men; A-men.

> Lord, we thank you; Lord, we thank you
> For this day, for this day.
> You have made us happy; you have made us happy.
> > A-men; A-men.

> Lord, we thank you; Lord, we thank you
> For our church, for our church.
> To worship and serve you, to worship and serve you.
> > A-men; A-men.

> Lord, we thank you; Lord, we thank you
> For your Word, for your Word.
> We can read of Jesus and his friends who knew him.
> > A-men; A-men.

Other Musical Expressions

Singing is not the only way to combine music and prayer. Music can be the backbone of meditative prayer. Recorded instrumental music is best for this because thoughts are not interrupted by someone else's words. As you hear music that might be appropriate to use as a background for prayer, make a note of it. Where possible, collect tapes and CDs that you can have available.

Instrumental music is also appropriate for movement prayers. I have a recording that I have used for more than thirty-five years with movement prayers. The recording is no longer available for sale, but fortunately I have two tapes of it—one for using and one for saving. It was too valuable a resource to risk being lost.

All children, even if they are hesitant in singing, will respond to accompanying themselves or a recording with musical instruments. These do not need to be purchased instruments. They may be simple instruments you make. Consider these suggestions:

Rhythm Sticks   Use one-half- to one-inch dowels for the sticks, and cut them in nine- to twelve-inch lengths. Decorate the sticks with colored markers or paints. A coat of varnish will keep the decoration bright even with use. The sticks may be used for instruments by hitting them together and hitting them on the floor.

Wrist or Ankle Bells   A set of bells may be made by attaching "jingle bells" to a band of one-inch elastic (black elastic is more practical). The bells may be attached by sewing or pinning them on with large safety pins. The bells can be used by shaking the wrist or ankle.

Drums   There are various articles that can be used for drums, from an oatmeal box to a large commercial size tin can to a wooden bucket to a small keg. Clay flower pots of graduating sizes may be used to produce different tones. Bottles or glasses may be filled with different amounts of water, thereby creating different tones when tapped lightly.

Shakers   Several items may be used in the manner of tambourines. Place small stones, buttons, or acorns between two aluminum pie tins or two hard plastic cups and tape the tins or cups together. These items may also be placed in a box or covered tin can. In some areas of the country, you may find seed pods that rattle when they have dried.

Sand Blocks   Select two blocks of wood the same size. For children, two by four by four (2x4x4) inches is an appropriate size. Cut coarse sandpaper about an inch larger than the blocks and place it on one side of the block, folding the ends over the edge and tacking or stapling them securely. The blocks are rubbed together to make a swishing sound.

Chapter 11

And Pray for Your Children and Youth

So we've thought of a variety of ways we can help children and youth pray creatively. Some methods will be more appealing to the particular children and youth you work with than others; some methods will appeal to you as a teacher more than others. Since prayer is so personal, it is not really measurable. A seed you plant today may bear its greatest fruit when the child is an adult.

Marlene Halpin, who is mentioned in an earlier chapter, was a Dominican sister who developed a prayer room at St. Augustine's School in Kalamazoo, Michigan, where children beginning at age five learned to pray contemplatively. In *Puddles of Knowing*, she reflected on the productivity of prayer.

Probably nothing is more anti-cultural than prayer. What are we educating for? Productivity. "What do you do?" is a question readily asked of a new acquaintance. In school, work has to be done. At home, work has to be done. At work, work has to be done. In any organization, work has to be done. We need to have something to show what we have done.

Not so in prayer. In prayer we are with God. That is enough. We do not produce anything. Nor are we graded. There is no way to compete, be rated, or have a score which is better or worse than another person's. There is not even a way to compete with ourselves and surpass our own past performance. That is anti-cultural! We have nothing to show for it—in a tangible, immediate sense.[1]

Of primary importance is the manner in which we help children and youth with their experiences of prayer. We must put opportunities before them in order for them to grow in their relationship with God and to pray in a natural way. But we cannot do that effectively if we ourselves do not have a prayer relationship with God. You may be able to teach children and youth "book learning" by reading from a book, and you may be able to introduce them to another person when you only know that person slightly. But prayer is different. Prayer is something that we must experience in order to effectively help others understand it. We must have sat and looked into the face of God if we are to effectively help others find their place in prayer. We cannot share an experience with enthusiasm unless we have been a part of that experience.

Let me suggest that you begin a prayer journal. Purchase a lined notebook that is the size of a Bible, or one of the bound books that are available with lines for writing. Keep it with your devotional materials, and set aside a special time each day to spend with God. Use the notebook not in the way you would a diary, but rather as a "conversation" with God. Begin your conversation by inviting God into your heart, then simply "looking and loving." As you wonder over God's greatness, write your thoughts into your prayer journal. Then begin to bring persons and situations into your heart, sharing them with God. The thoughts and feelings that come out of this experience can be written into your prayer journal, too. Be sure to include the students in your prayer. Use the prayer calendar model that is printed on page 11 of this book.

I have used a prayer journal for several years now, sometimes more regularly than at other times. I've never reread most of the pages, and I may never reread them. But just writing the thoughts down helped with my praying process. My prayer journal is not like my other writings in which I write, read, and rewrite. I don't have to worry about grammar or spelling. I don't even have to write it so that others can read it! Instead, I write to help process my thoughts. The experience at the time is what counts. Writing the conversations with God helps me to come closer to God. It helps me draw God into my everyday life.

As your prayer life deepens, you will be better able to guide children and youth into the God/person relationship that we call prayer.

If I pray eloquent prayers of my church to my children,
    but do not pray myself,
        I am a noisy gong or a clanging symbol.
And if I lead children and youth through steps of prayer preparation,
    but do not take time to talk with God myself,
        I am nothing.
If I place before children and youth materials for them to use
    in creating their own prayers,
But only mouth memorized prayers myself,
    I gain nothing.
Prayer is communication with God,
But I cannot lead others into communication
    if I only speak lines as if in a drama.
Prayers of our heritage, prayer patterns, creative activities,
    these profit me none,
Unless I spend time with God myself,
    one on one,
        simply lookin' and lovin'.

Notes

1. What Is Prayer and How Do We Begin?

1. Delia T. Halverson, *How Do Our Children Grow?* (St. Louis: Chalice Press, 1999), p. 74.

2. Lance Webb, *The Art of Personal Prayer* (Nashville: Abingdon Press, 1962), pp. 97-98.

6. Spontaneous Prayer

1. As told by Dr. Millie Goodson, Associate Professor of Christian Education, Scarritt Graduate School, Nashville, Tennessee.

7. Creating Personal Prayers

1. Delia Halverson, *Living Simply* (Nashville: Abingdon Press, 1996), pp. 111-12. (See Ron DelBene with Herb and Mary Montgomery, *When I'm Alone* [Nashville: The Upper Room, 1988], pp. 7-9.)

8. Creating Group Prayers

1. Delia Halverson, *Grades 5-6 Teacher, Vacation Bible School* (Nashville: Graded Press, 1987), p. 48.

11. And Pray for Your Children and Youth

1. Marlene Halpin, *Puddles of Knowing* (Dubuque, Iowa: William C. Brown Company, 1984), p. 47.

Resource List

For Adults

Cloyd, Betty Shannon. *Children and Prayer*. Nashville: The Upper Room, 1997.

Connell, Jane, and Nancy Spence. *From BC to PC: A Guide for Using Computers with Children in Christian Education*. Nashville: Abingdon Press, 1998.

DelBene, Ron. *The Hunger of the Heart*. Nashville: Discipleship Resources, 1992.

Dunnam, Maxie. *Workbook of Living Prayer*. Nashville: Discipleship Resources, 1974.

Foster, Richard. *Prayer: Finding the Heart's True Home*. San Francisco: HarperCollins Publishers, 1992.

Halpin, Marlene. *Puddles of Knowing*. Dubuque, Iowa: William C. Brown, 1984.

Halverson, Delia T. *How Do Our Children Grow?* St. Louis: Chalice Press, 1999.

———. *Side by Side: Families Learning and Living the Faith Together*. Nashville: Abingdon Press, 2002.

———. *Teaching and Celebrating the Christian Seasons*. St. Louis: Chalice Press, 2002.

Ingram, Kristen Johnson. *Family Worship Through the Year*. Valley Forge, Pa.: Judson Press, 1984.

Job, Rueben, and Norman Shawchuck. *Guide to Prayer for All God's People*. Nashville: The Upper Room, 1994.

Kichenburger, James. *Fun Devotions for Parents and Teenagers*. Loveland, Colo.: Group Publishing, 1990.

MacQueen, Neil. *Computers, Kids, and Christian Education*. Minneapolis: Augsburg Fortress, 1998.

Terrell, Charles. *Hey, God, Let's Talk!* (leader's manual). Nashville: Abingdon Press, 2000.

Webb, Lance. *The Art of Personal Prayer*. Nashville: Abingdon Press, 1992.

Younger, Barbara. *Sing It, Make It, Say It, Pray It*. Nashville: Abingdon Press, 2003.

For Children and Youth

Barclay, William. *Prayers for Young People.* Nashville: Abingdon Press, 1993.

———. *More Prayers for Young People.* Nashville: Abingdon Press, 1993.

Brown, Susan. *Can I Pray with My Eyes Open?* New York: Hyperion Books, 1999.

Caswell, Helen. *I Can Talk with God.* Nashville: Abingdon Press, 1989.

Devo'Zine. A youth devotional. Nashville: The Upper Room, P.O. Box 340009, Nashville, TN 37202-0009.

Gilliam, Lynn, and Janet Knight. *My Journal: A Place to Write About God and Me.* Nashville: The Upper Room, 1997.

Hardesty, Brian. *Closer to God: Prayer Journal.* Nashville: Abingdon Press, 1997.

Koch, Carl (ed.). *Dreams Alive: Prayers by Teenagers.* Winona, Minn.: St. Mary's Press, 1991.

Neinast, Helen R., and Thomas C. Ettinger. *What About God? Now That You're Off to College: A Prayer Guide.* Nashville: The Upper Room, 1994.

Pockets. A devotional periodical. The Upper Room, P.O. Box 340009, Nashville, TN 37202-0009.

Sasso, Sandy Eisenberg. *In God's Name.* Woodstock, Vt.: Jewish Lights Publishing, 1994.

Swanson, Steve. *Faith Prints: Youth Devotions for Every Day of the Year.* Minneapolis: Augsburg Fortress, 1990.

Terrell, Charles. *Hey, God, Let's Talk!* Children's prayer journal. Nashville: Abingdon Press, 2000.

Willis, Doris. *We Give Thanks!* Nashville: Abingdon Press, 1991.

Curriculum and Media Resources

About Prayer—A Coloring and Activities Book. Scriptographic Booklet. South Deerfield, Mass., 1984.

Borgstadt, Chip. *Growing Spiritually.* Youth Search—Small Group Resources Series. Nashville: Abingdon Press, 1996.

Hardesty, Brian. *Closer to God: Youth Experiencing Prayer.* Nashville: Abingdon Press, 1997.

McKinnon, Greg. *Helping Youth Pray: How to Connect Youth with God.* Nashville: Abingdon Press, 1997.

PowerXpress: Teach Us How to Pray. Nashville: Abingdon Press, 2003.

Pray and Play Songs for Young Children. Audiocassette. Loveland, Colo.: Group Publishing, 1997.

Psalm Prayer. Five filmstrips and cassette tapes of Psalms. Treehaus Communications, PO Box 249 Loveland, OH 45140.

Teach Us to Pray. Grades 2-6 elective unit: six basic one-hour sessions with suggestions for expanding sessions. Teacher/student books. Nashville: Graded Press, 1985.

Teaching Children About Prayer, by Judy Gattis Smith. Five sessions for elementary children. Prescott, Ariz.: Educational Ministries, Inc., 1988.